Hidden Treasure

What people are saying about *Hidden Treasure*

"*The book itself a treasure, as it recounts the story of Potter's House and their care for the Treasures. Gladys allows us to see not just what Potter's House was able to do, but what God has done in her and in many through the entire story of the garbage dump in Guatemala City. This book will both inspire you to keep your eyes open to God's working and challenge you to see the things that you might usually ignore. Not only that, it will instruct you to better understand the layers and complexity of poverty and addressing those issues from a Christian worldview. Read this book, and then share it with others!*"

Justin Burkholder
Regional Executive Director, Americas
TEAM

"*I met Gladys Acuña Güitz about 15 years ago and was immediately impressed by the depth of her dependence on God, her humility and grace. This book gives the reader a bird's eye view of the work God has done and is doing at Potter's House. Gladys, with candid openness, lets you into her heart, sharing the struggles, the joys, the questions and the lessons learned. To me, she is a hero of the faith, constantly pointing me to the greatness of our God.*"

Shanthini Baskaran
Board Member
Potter's House Association International

"The story of how God brought Potter's House into being is truly inspirational. It challenges readers to step out of their comfort zones and open their eyes to what He may be doing in, around and through them if only they will trust Him. *Hidden Treasure* is a testimony of the power of God to use the ordinary to do extraordinary things."

Susan Hutton
Mendham Hills Community Church

"*Hidden Treasure* tells the story of one woman's humble faith that let her to follow God, experience His heart for the poor and discover her calling in the Guatemala City garbage dump among the Treasures that she would come to love dearly. Gladys opens her heart to share her struggles and misconceptions, as well as the deeper understandings she has gained about God, herself and others. I was drawn into each chapter and inspired to learn from the lessons of faith, adversity and God's gracious and timely provision.

Gladys's journey is filled with practical understanding about God's love for people expressed in tangible ways through a wholistic ministry that has remained Christ-centered for more than three decades. You will find *Hidden Treasure* to be both insightful and inspiring."

Rick Lowe
Executive Director
Shepherds' Support International

Cover Design by Klassic Designs
Interior design and formatting by Nelly Murariu at pixbeedesign.com

Hidden Treasure

Finding God in Unexpected Places

Gladys Acuña Güitz

with Betsy Ahl

Acknowledgments

God has promised to give me every good thing I need to do His will. I always knew that was true, but writing this book confirmed it to me as never before. Thank you, Lord, for trusting me to write Your story and to be part of building Your Kingdom in Guatemala.

As I look back on that story, I see that He gave me parents who dedicated my life to God, putting me in His hands, trusting in His plans. They showed me with their lives how to follow and serve Jesus. He provided brothers and sisters, nieces and nephews who have shaped my life. The generation of those nieces and nephews will continue to bring light to the world.

After many years of praying, the Lord answered those prayers when He brought my husband, Edgar, the love of my life and my partner in adventure and ministry for 25 years. He has believed in me and encouraged me to be obedient with everything the Lord has entrusted to me, and this book is part of that. He provided valuable insights into this book. My life would not be the same without him.

I also acknowledge and thank God for my spiritual mother and mentor, Beatriz Zapata Espinoza, who walked alongside me when I most needed it.

Another friend and supporter from the early days is Dr. Samuel Berberian. He walked alongside us as a board member in Guatemala when we had just started following God's path toward serving the Treasures, trusting us and guiding us gently with his wisdom.

I also thank Him for Betsy Ahl, who walked with me through the process of writing His story, using her knowledge of English to help make my experience understandable and interesting to international readers. Now I understand why God prepared her as an editor for just such a time as this.

I would not have been able to do this without the prayer warrior team that prayed and supported this project and held up my hands.

Without the assistance of the FlourishWriters Ministry, this book would not have been possible. They provided me with all the tools I needed to give birth to God's story.

My friends Jim and Ruth Youngman, Rick Lowe, Shanthini Baskaran, Justin Burkholder, Héctor Rivas, Susie Hutton and Daniel Anderson encouraged me and provided feedback and insights into this book.

The thousands of courageous men and women who have served alongside me as staff, board members and volunteers at Potter's House and helped build His kingdom in Guatemala since 1986 are a big part of His story!

Finally, I acknowledge my dear Treasures, who have been my mentors and my friends in the process of finding God in unexpected places.

Contents

Foreword

Potter's House and the Treasures of the Guatemala City garbage dump changed my life.

It started innocently enough at a missions conference at Mendham Hills Community Church in Northern New Jersey back in the mid-1990's. Seated next to my Venezuelan friend Carolina Bonet, I was inspired by the message of a man who had been a missionary to Africa for many years. Don't misunderstand; I was inspired on behalf of others who I thought should do God's work on the mission field. I knew I would never allow myself to face the privations the speaker described, and that, furthermore, I would be poor missionary.

Not so Carolina. At the end of the service, she leaned over and said to me, "When Mendham Hills has a mission trip, we're going to go!" I, knowing that the church, although part of the Christian & *Missionary* Alliance, had never sponsored a mission trip, replied without enthusiasm, "Sure."

About ten years later, in 2005, the chairman of the Mendham Hills Missions Team announced that the church was going to be taking a team of volunteers to Guatemala to work among the scavengers who relied on the Guatemala City garbage dump for their livelihood. Once again, Carolina was seated beside me. She leaned over and whispered excitedly, "This is so wonderful! We're finally going on a mission trip!"

By the time church was over, she had already started making plans—for *us!* "Wait just a minute!" I said. "Did you not hear that they're going to a *garbage dump*?! I don't want to do that."

Her reply was simple and compelling: "But you promised." And I had, so we both signed up. A few weeks later, my husband, Dave, decided to join us.

In the weeks leading up to the trip, we received very little information about what we would be doing in Guatemala. We knew that our host was a Guatemalan ministry called Potter's House that was located on the edge of that garbage dump. We also knew that Potter's House had an Education Program for the scavengers' children.

"Aha!" I thought. "I have studied Spanish. I can help the teachers learn English! Then I won't have to go near the garbage." I shared my plan with God, who gave me no indication that He endorsed it. Nevertheless, I continued to plot. There had to be a way a middle-aged gringa could serve Him without getting her hands dirty.

When we finally arrived at Potter's House, we were told that we had two projects. We were to pour concrete floors in three shacks near the dump and paint the immense, new multi-purpose room that was four stories of raw concrete block. Whew! I quickly signed up to paint and did so contentedly for the rest of the first day.

On the second day, the team leader announced that we were to change places. The painters were to go outside and pour concrete and yesterday's concrete-pourers were to become today's painters. Oh NO!

I dragged my bad attitude out into the community where our team was working, and within 20 minutes I was hooked. The people were friendly, charming and grateful for what we were doing. The children were adorable, waiting to throw their arms around their new American friends. All the adults whose houses we worked on pitched in to help, and even some of the children did what they could. One young girl, Fabiola, worked tirelessly, transporting sand down the narrow alley in a battered wheelbarrow. One of our volunteers fell in love, started sponsoring her and continued to support her all the way through high school. The last time I saw Fabiola, she was working as a receptionist at Potter's House, the first member of her family to graduate from high school.

The next year, our pastor asked me to take over the preparations and logistics for the trip. That year we had 36 volunteers—most of them veterans from the year before—and built several concrete-block houses in the dump community.

I mentioned above that I had studied Spanish. Well, I actually majored in it in college and taught it for a couple years. But once I decided that high school teaching wasn't for me and pursued a career in publishing, I never had occasion to use my Spanish again. From time to time, I would ask God what that was all about. Why had He led me to major in a language that was to play no part in my life for three decades?

It took a trip to a garbage dump for me to see God's long-term plan. I am now the executive director of Beyond the Walls, the secular nonprofit we created to do fund-raising and attract volunteers from other churches and faiths. (See Chapter 16, Exchange of Blessings, for more on Beyond the Walls.) I normally spend three or four weeks a year in Guatemala, and in 2009 I lived there for three months, working at Potter's House. It's easy for me to say that Guatemala is my adoptive home.

The gringa who didn't want to get her hands dirty now knows hundreds of the scavengers whom Potter's House calls "Treasures" and hugs them joyfully in the Guatemalan way every time she sees them in the community.

Some of my dearest friends (including Gladys Acuña Güitz, the author of this book) are Guatemalans who work or have worked at Potter's House. The way they live their Christian lives, depending on God as they make even the smallest decisions, has inspired me to take my own faith much more seriously. I have spent countless hours in the homes of the Treasures, listening to their stories and praying for their overwhelming needs. They have shown me first-hand the power of prayer, which has helped me to improve my prayer life. Guatemala is the place where I feel closest to God—and most capable of being the hands and feet of Jesus.

I still need a lot of improvement, but I am a better person because of Potter's House and its Treasures. I am living proof of the truth of the Beyond the Walls tag line: The life you change could be your own!

Betsy Ahl
Executive Director
Beyond the Walls
Beyond-the-walls.org

Introduction

Has anyone ever asked you for a favor that you *really* didn't want to do? If so, you know how I felt at the start of this story.

I was asked to do a favor in a dirty, smelly, dangerous place—on Christmas Eve! I did it reluctantly and breathed a sigh of relief when it was over, telling myself that I would never return to that awful place.

But I soon learned that God had other ideas. His plan was that a garbage dump would shape the rest of my life. That one act of obedience—doing a favor for some friends—set my feet on a path that had nothing to do with the plans I had for my own life. I thought I knew what His will for me was, and I did not hesitate to point that out to Him. My plan, I reminded Him, was to get a Ph.D. in psychology so people would call me "Dr. Gladys." But God continued to surprise me; "Dr. Gladys" was not part of His plan.

His path led me to some very unexpected places—places in which I would never have thought to look for Him. His path led me to friendships with people I never even knew existed prior to doing that favor. His path led me to start a ministry that has endured for more than three decades—a ministry that has impacted the lives of not only those friends but hundreds of international friends whose lives have been changed by finding God in some very unexpected places.

His path led me to a deeper understanding of His heart for the poor. His word is full of verses that encourage us to love and serve the poor as if we were serving Him directly. It sounds easy, but it was very challenging for me.

His path even led me to my husband, despite warnings from my friends that I would never find a suitable man if I continued to serve in a garbage dump.

When I set out on this journey, I thought I was poor, because I defined poverty as lack of resources, and my family had very few material resources. I eventually came to realize that poverty is much more than lack of resources. The Lord led the Potter's House team to identify *eight* forms of poverty and set a goal of finding ways to address them all. When you get to Chapters 9 and 10, you will learn about those eight forms of poverty and how we continue to fight them.

After I understood my calling, all I ever wanted was to serve the poor in the name of Jesus with all my heart. I had no idea it would be so complicated to achieve what seemed to be such a simple goal.

Another thing that I learned along the way was that I was not the potter—the designer and creator of my own life. God is the Potter—in my life and yours. Like a potter, He does not throw out the original clay that has been scarred and misshapen by circumstances and mistakes. He does not waste the pain we experience; He takes it into He gentle but firm hands and shapes our lives, molding us into beautiful, priceless pieces of art that bring glory to Him.

Where and how is God is shaping you? Are you brave enough to put yourself in His hands and allow Him to transform you?

Finally, this is God's story. I invite you to join me on the journey. Find God in unexpected places. Find your *Hidden Treasure* and learn how you can change the world—one person at a time.

To my husband, who I found
in an unexpected place!

CHAPTER 1

It All Began With A Favor

Christmas, a joyful celebration for most people, has always been a difficult, emotional time for me. It was Christmas when God called my mother, who was only 42-years old, home to be with Him. For a girl of 15, the loss was extremely painful, and that pain led me to start questioning God. Why hadn't He answered my prayers for healing? I was a teenager; didn't He know how much I needed my mom?

But instead of having a mom, I *became* a mom, helping my dad to raise my sister and four brothers. The Lord provided a very special father—a faithful man with a good sense of humor who taught us to trust God through pain and loss. My parents were second-generation Christians, and even though we were poor, living on limited resources, they provided each of their six children with two priceless gifts: a college education and, even more important, the example of a deep and abiding relationship with Jesus, our Savior. I learned to follow Jesus at a young age and continued to do so in adulthood.

It was many years later, in 1986, once again at Christmas, when some friends from the States who had visited me in Guatemala asked my friend Lisbeth Piedrasanta and me for a favor. I didn't know it at the time, but God was about to redeem my lingering, painful memories of Christmas by giving me an opportunity that would change my life.

My friends from the states had visited Guatemala City and learned its dirty little secret—at the geographic center of the capital city there was a community of people who relied entirely on a giant garbage dump for their livelihood. Struck by the poverty and pain they saw there, the Americans asked us to buy blankets and give them as Christmas gifts in the name of Jesus to the people who scavenged in that dump.

Although I was a Christian who believed in serving others, I was not enthusiastic about this request. I wanted to spend Christmas at home, wearing my new dress and enjoying my family. We would celebrate Jesus' birth together and at the same time comfort one another as we remembered our precious mother. The last place I wanted to be was a dirty, smelly, dangerous garbage dump, surrounded by dirty, smelly, dangerous people, most of whom didn't even have beds on which to put those blankets.

God's Timing

So Lisbeth and I asked the man in charge of delivering the blankets to bring them two days before Christmas. Surely Jesus wouldn't mind if we gave out His gifts a day or two early. Our chosen delivery date came and went. Likewise, the following day

Surely Jesus wouldn't mind if we gave out His gifts a day or two early.

passed without a blanket in sight. Finally, they arrived late in the day on Christmas Eve. We were going to have to put on our old clothes, leave our families, and distribute blankets on Christmas day—exactly the way God had planned. For years I have been telling people that those blankets arrived in God's time, not Gladys's time.

In addition to being resentful about the timing of the project, I was nervous—frightened even. I had never been in the garbage dump, but I believed the rumors that said it was a dangerous place. Like most of the city's inhabitants, I believed that the useful life of my food, clothing, and other discards ended in a garbage can at the curb. I never knew that for many of my fellow Guatemalans, the trucks that collected that refuse and took it to the largest sanitary landfill in Central America were just the beginning.

We had 350 blankets, and Lisbeth and I were afraid that without a plan we might be mobbed by the scavengers and possibly hurt or killed. So we found a church about a block from the dump and asked the pastor to keep the van containing the blankets while we went into the dump to give out 350 tickets that would entitle the holders to one blanket each.

As we approached the garbage dump, I was revolted by the stench—the stench of the more than 3,200 tons of waste deposited daily into a ravine as big as 24 American football fields. The acrid smell reminded me of the fumes issuing from a well-used garbage pail on a hot day. Not only did it make us gag, but it clung to our clothes long after we left the dump area. The garbage trucks were bright yellow box trucks with a hydraulic mechanism that raised the box and dumped the garbage they had collected from homes around the city. As they drove to the day's dumping site, their exhaust mixed with thick clouds of dust that enveloped the scavengers running behind them with their bags and sticks, eager to get the best garbage from each truck. The air was dirty and polluted. No wonder, as I later learned, they suffered from severe respiratory ailments.

Not surprisingly, the people were just as filthy as their surroundings. Without the luxury of plentiful running water in their homes, the scavengers were encrusted with dirt. Their layers of clothes, which had been pulled from the dump weeks or months earlier were tattered and stained. Their worn-out shoes offered little protection from broken glass, jagged metal shards, rusty nails and other dangerous debris.

To be honest, I didn't even want to get close to the scavengers or touch them. But then I looked around and saw children digging in the garbage, playing in the garbage, sleeping in the garbage. Tiny babies were lying in boxes near where their mothers were working. Mangy, scrawny dogs were everywhere. It was too much for me, and I promised myself I would never return to this place. All I had to do was survive the distribution process, and I could return home and forget about this hell on earth.

Trying to Forget

We returned to the church, followed by the people who had received the tickets. With the help of the pastor, we started giving out the blankets. The scavengers' filthy faces reflected the suffering in their bodies and hearts. I averted my eyes whenever possible, and soon we were done. I went home, put on my new Christmas dress, spent time with my family, and tried to forget what I had seen.

While I was trying to forget, Lisbeth was already looking ahead to next year.

Lisbeth and I talked about the experience the next day when we saw each other at the Christian counseling center where we worked. While I was trying to forget, Lisbeth was already looking ahead to next year. "Why don't we have a Christmas celebration in the dump again next year?" she asked.

What could I say? We were close friends and Christians are commanded to serve the poor. We agreed to return to the dump the following year for an even bigger Christmas celebration.

A year later, we returned with a celebration for 1,000 people— 500 children and 500 adults. We gave out blankets and shared the gospel and the meaning of Christmas. After that, we served hundreds of tamales, the typical Guatemalan celebration food.

That second Christmas celebration was such a success that we decided to do it the following year for 2,000 people and the next year for 3,000 people. By then I realized that I was beginning to learn how to be the hands and feet of Jesus, smiling at and embracing the poorest of the poor with His love.

After several years of hosting Christmas celebrations in the garbage dump, Lisbeth and I were astounded to discover how many families lived and worked in the communities surrounding the dump—communities that had sprung up on reclaimed land around the edges of the landfill. Delivering one meal, one blanket, one Bible study a year was not enough. We felt a tug on our hearts; we wanted to do something to meet the everyday needs of our new friends.

I grew up thinking I was poor, but God used the people of the garbage dump to open my eyes to how richly blessed I really was. In the past, I had not been concerned about the poor, because I thought I was one of them. Now I realized that Jesus wanted me to serve them and give all the credit for what I accomplished to God.

Neither Lisbeth nor I knew anything about working with people living in such appalling circumstances. There were so many needs; where should we start? I started questioning my theology, just as I had when my mom died. Did God really care for these scavengers? If so, why did He allow them to live in such awful poverty? Did Jesus really have the power to change their lives? If so, what was the best way to introduce Him to them?

We had seen the Lord provide miraculously for our Christmas celebrations, but at the same time, we started to see just how dire the needs of our friends were. We decided to bring my Sunday school class to the dump community every Saturday to have Bible classes with the children in the same church from which we had distributed the original blankets.

From those Saturday Bible classes grew what would become the Potter's House Education Program—a program that would help educate the school-age children of the scavengers and teach their parents the value of education, a program that would offer children of scavengers an opportunity to graduate from high school and even attend college in the years to come.

It was very painful for me to be in the garbage dump that first Christmas. I saw children playing in the trash, others were sniffing glue, and some were even digging for food in the garbage. I told to myself, "I will never return; this was a one-time favor."

More than 34 years later, I can say that the most beautiful years of my life were spent in that dump.

> *He will help the poor when they cry out and*
> *will save the needy when no one else will help.*
> *He will be kind to the weak and poor, and he*
> *will save their lives.*—**Psalm 72:12-13 (CEV)**

Personal or Group Follow-Up

Would you have agreed to do the favor that Gladys and Lisbeth were asked to do? Why or why not?

↔

In what ways do you believe that God cares for the poor?

↔

What "favors" have you been asked to do that resulted in something more significant than you first thought?

↔

Where are the uncomfortable places in your life to which God has been prompting you to go?

CHAPTER 2

Cristo Vive!

Cristo vive! (Christ lives!) It was the shout of 200 children after a solemn prayer at a megachurch of about 4,000 people on a Sunday morning. The response startled the congregation in their pews; it was not part of the program. But within seconds, they responded in unison, "Amen! Amen!"

That moment was like the voice of a great multitude in heaven proclaiming and celebrating that Christ is alive. How did it come about?

As we got to know the Treasures, we learned that most of them had just two concepts of Jesus—concepts that are prevalent throughout Latin culture. First was the baby Jesus, during the Christmas season—usually a figurine of Jesus wrapped in swaddling clothes lying in a manger. The second was the crucified Jesus, during the Easter season—the crucifix that symbolized Jesus dying on the cross.

Neither of these concepts of Jesus, was relevant to the lives of the people in the community. A baby cannot help me; on the contrary, a baby needs my help. A crucified Jesus is half-dead; he cannot help me either. Maybe he needs my help too. With those two figures of Jesus dominating the worldview of the people, how could we show them a Jesus that was relevant to their lives?

We began to be very intentional in our descriptions of God and Jesus Son of God, teaching about the Jesus who came to earth in love to live the beauty and tragedy of the human life, the resurrected Jesus who is above all names and will come again, the loving and all-powerful Jesus who is relevant to every aspect of our lives here and now—our only hope for eternal life.

To remind the Treasures of that truth, at Potter's House, after every prayer, we declared with conviction: Cristo Vive!

Once the Treasures realized that Jesus Christ was alive in them and they made the decision to embark upon a personal relationship with Him, the confession of "Cristo Vive!" reminded them that Jesus is neither a baby nor a dead man.

When we understand that Christ lives, seeing the world through His eyes changes how we live. Without that important piece, Christianity is just a religion. Even though I grew up in a Christian home, I had never understood the difference between religiosity and the Christian life.

Religiosity attempts to control a relationship while Jesus grants freedom.

There is a vast difference between man's religion and a genuine relationship with Christ. I am not talking about denominations of churches. I am talking about religion that relies on our attempts to reach God by our own efforts. Religiosity attempts to control a relationship while Jesus grants freedom.

As the Treasures began to know Jesus, we wanted to help them to continue growing in community in relationship with others as Hebrews 10:24 encourages us. We all need others as we seek to grow, love and support others in times of need, practice our God-given spiritual gifts and serve others. But where would we find such a community for the Treasures?

The first thing I did was ask my pastor if we could bring 200 children from the garbage dump area to my small, local church. Sadly, the answer was no. "We are not ready to receive them," he said. It was terrible to hear him say that. I felt as if my kids had been rejected.

That was my last day attending that church. I thanked them for the many years I was part of the congregation and decided to go where "my" kids were embraced and could grow in community.

God opened a door at that megachurch where 200 hundred kids would not be so obvious. So, we rented two buses, and every Sunday we left for church bright and early, taking some volunteers and parents with us.

The congregation received the Treasures with love and a lot of patience. The church leaders identified leaders among the Treasures and discipled them in small groups. Some of those Treasures continue attending and serving at the church that welcomed them so long ago and taught them how to live in community.

Experiencing the reactions of those two different churches to the little Treasures was one of my early encounters with what we would later call Spiritual Poverty: Religiosity vs. Christian life.

Reveal, Where are You?

Later, I would come across it again in a more structured presentation. In *Reveal, Where are You?* by Greg Hawkins and Cathy Parkinson I found the description of that dichotomy for which I had been searching.

In 2004, Hawkins and Parkinson, staff members at Willow Creek Community Church, working with Eric Arnson, a consumer research advisor, set out to gain a new understanding of the spiritual lives of their congregation

Their initial hypothesis was that the more the people got involved in church activities, the more they would grow in Christ. What they found were four levels of spiritual growth:

- ↬ Exploring Christianity
- ↬ Growing in Christ
- ↬ Close to Christ
- ↬ Christ-Centered

What they called "the brutal truth about spiritual growth" was that at the first two levels, the more a person grew in Christ, the more he or she focused on life within the four walls of the church (temple) when searching for opportunities to serve.

They also discovered that when people reached the Close-to-Christ and Christ-Centered levels, many became dissatisfied because the church did not provide enough opportunities to grow through service. Among the things they searched for were opportunities to serve the poor. I would add that they wanted to follow Jesus into unexpected places just as I had 20 years earlier.

Back then, I was living religiously, but my life was incomplete. I ignored God's command to serve the poor, focusing instead on activities within the church. I was content in my comfort zone, but I did not realize how much I was missing until God put me in challenging situations where I had to trust Him completely.

The paradox is that we find freedom when we commit our lives to the God we may once have thought would take away

The paradox is that we find freedom when we commit our lives to the God we may once have thought would take away our freedom.

our freedom. We find that freedom as we experience God, grow in Jesus and live in the Holy Spirit.

Once we start to live a full Christ-centered life, that life becomes exciting and meaningful as we begin to enjoy serving others. Jesus said in Matthew 20:28, "In the same way, the Son of Man did not come to be served. He came to serve others and to give his life as a ransom for many people." (NCV)

Christianity is a religion, but when we stop being "religious" and start conscientiously following Christ and serving God, Christianity becomes integrated into every aspect of our lives—everything we do. Try as we might, we cannot ignore His leading. It becomes second nature to consult with Him at every decision point—no matter how small—in our lives.

I learned that He wanted me to obey His command to serve the poor no matter how uncomfortable or unprepared I felt.

Having left religiosity behind, I can confidently assure the Treasures that Jesus is not just a baby or a person who lived a long time ago. Every day, we celebrate the Resurrection because Jesus Christ is alive and real in our lives, and we celebrate what God wants to do in our lives.

Indeed, Cristo Vive! Christ lives!

If you declare with your mouth, "Jesus is Lord,"
and believe in your heart that God raised him
from the dead, you will be saved.—**Romans 10:9**

Personal or Group Follow-Up

What does declaring "Christ Lives!" mean to you?

✎

How being a person who has a relationship with Christ different from being a religious person? Which are you?

✎

Are you willing to follow Jesus into unexpected places? Where might those be?

✎

Is there room in your community of faith for people different from you?

Additional Resources

Reveal: Where Are You? Greg L. Hawkins and Cally Parkinson. Willow Creek Association. 2007.

The Jesus I Never Knew. Philip Yancey. Zondervan. 2007.

CHAPTER 3

The Journey of Our Trash

Have you ever thought that the life of your stuff might not end in your garbage pail? I certainly never did. But on my first visit to the dump in 1986, I realized that in Guatemala City, a city of 3 million inhabitants, much of our trash starts a new life in the dark, stinky reaches of our garbage pails.

I was surprised to learn that our capital city nearly 11,000 people (most of them children), lived in and around the largest landfill in Central America. It was known as *el basurero*—the dump.

Approximately 550 garbage trucks collected garbage from the capital city and surrounding towns and deposited 500 tons of waste each day into a ravine the size of about 24 American football fields. The results were terrible pollution and the foul odor of garbage permeating the atmosphere. Most of Guatemala City's inhabitants believed that this was where it all ended, but the daily deliveries to the city dump were just the beginning for many.

Those were the people, who searched desperately for scraps to help them survive. The dump was no respecter of age or gender; men, women, teens, and even children toiled amid the mountains of waste, surrounded by the filth and stench of rotting garbage.

They were contemptuously called "scavengers" because their work consisted of scavenging through the disgusting rubbish, collecting bits of plastic, cardboard, glass, or metal—any item they could sell, something that could be recycled, or a lucky piece of food to satisfy their hunger for the day. Competition for the best refuse was stiff among the scavengers themselves, but they also had to compete with the clouds of vultures that were always soaring overhead. It was brutal job, but it was a job, and it helped them support their families.

After 14 hours of grueling work in the harsh sun or pouring rain, scavenging among sharp objects and highly toxic materials, these people would sell their day's findings for an average of about US$5. They returned home caked with dust and dirt, the skin on their hands cracked and bloody. This was not just poverty; this was utter misery!

As the ravine filled up around the edges, the municipality would cover it with a layer of sand, and eager scavengers would move in, staking their claims on land that they hoped would years later be deeded over to them by the city government and creating de facto communities.

Their parents had been scavengers and their children could aspire to nothing else.

Families were born and raised in the dump communities, caught in the cycle of generational poverty. Their parents had been scavengers and their children could aspire to nothing else. Some had lived for decades in shacks made of cardboard and sheet metal without so much as a hose to supply running water. As they scavenged and struggled for each day's sustenance there was no room for hope, no reason to look forward to a brighter future.

Even though they live, work, and find food in the garbage, we do not consider them to be trash. In our eyes, they are God's beloved Treasures—as valuable as any other person He has created. At Potter's House, Scavengers are valued as Treasures.

Created in God's Image

I have learned at Potter's House that God never intended His greatest creation to live and work amid the refuse cast off by their neighbors. That is just not acceptable—to Him or to us. Ephesians 2:10 says, "For we are God's masterpiece. He has created us anew in Christ Jesus so that we can do the good things He planned for us long ago." (NLT)

At Potter's House, we believe that even though the scavengers live and work in the dump, they are not garbage; they are treasures. They are human beings with value and dignity. We have called them Treasures because they are not trash; they are God's creation, made in His image.

We believe that each of them is precious in the sight of God and that each of them deserves to be treated with dignity and respect as a beloved child for whom He sent His Son to die so that they might have eternal life with Him. In Psalm 113:7-8, we learn that God has a special heart for the poor: *"God lifts the poor and needy from the garbage dump, he sets them among princes, even the princes of His own people." (NLT)* God lets them take part in ruling His people.

Working at Potter's House and becoming more and more involved in the lives of the Treasures, we began to see them as God sees them. Despite the challenging working conditions and the high risk to their health from the pervasive pollution, the staff at Potter's House remains committed to serving the Treasures in the name of Jesus. Our goal is to show them His love in action.

Kids Sniffing Glue

In the early days, among the Treasures who came to our program was a group of boys and one girl who were sniffing glue—a cheap way to get high. We did some investigation and learned that glue-sniffers risk respiratory problems and damage to the nervous system, especially the brain. Getting high kept their minds off their empty stomachs and allowed them to ignore the hopelessness around them but put their health in serious jeopardy.

This group came every day for the lunch program. As I got to know them and heard their stories, my heart was touched, and I began to see them not as unfortunate children making bad decisions but as human beings created by God—human beings just like me.

My mind was filled with questions. I poured out my heart before God asking Him to change those kids. Every night when I returned home, I would go straight to bed. All I wanted to do was close my eyes and forget about the misery I had seen during the day. I felt guilty for having a home and food to eat—so guilty that I refused to buy anything for myself during those first years.

But God in His mercy showed me that I needed to learn to be content with my own circumstances. As Paul says in Philippians 4:11-12,

I began to be grateful for what God had given me and generous in sharing everything with which He had entrusted me.

"Not that I speak from want, for I have learned to be content in whatever circumstances I am. I know how to get along with humble means, and I also know how to live in prosperity;

in any and every circumstance, I have learned the secret of being filled and going hungry, both of having abundance and suffering need." (NASB 1995)

I began to be grateful for what God had given me and generous in sharing everything with which He had entrusted me—time, talent and treasure. It was devastating to watch those kids slowly ruining their lives. I found myself asking, "wouldn't it be better for them to die quickly instead of slowly and eventually painfully like this?"

Seven members of one family—six boys and a girl—were part of that group. They were beautiful with lovely dark eyes and sweet smiles. I wanted to know how they had become drug users. As they began to trust us, we learned that their mother would lock them all in the single room of their wood-and-tin shack while she scavenged in the garbage dump every day. When the two youngest cried because they were hungry, one of the older kids gave them the glue to sniff to dull their pain and keep them quiet.

Knowing that, we invited the two youngest ones to Potter's House. It was for them (and many others) an oasis—a place where they received a warm meal, a shower and love. We wanted not only to save their lives but to give them hope for a better future. The sweet-smelling soap cleaned their dirty hands and faces, and while they were with us we offered them the sweet hope of eternal salvation that would cleanse their hearts forever.

One day we received the sad news that their mother had died. Of course, our first thoughts were of the two children with whom we had been working. Who would take care of them? The older siblings, who were between 14 and 18 years old, were accustomed to fending for themselves. But what about the little ones?

I went to the mother's funeral, and after expressing my condolences, I asked a family member why she thought the mom had decided to move to the garbage dump community. Her relatives appeared to be a hard-working lower middle-class family; how had she ended up in that hopeless situation? I never got an answer to my questions. The relatives were as baffled as I was.

The family took the two youngest children, but the others said they preferred to stay in the dump community. Little-by-little, they stopped coming to our program. I looked for them, but I never saw them again.

Mynor's Story

Another boy who was part of the glue-sniffing group was Mynor Lopez, who worked in the garbage dump. He was 10-years old when he started to participate in the programs we offered in the early days of Potter's House. Even then he led a nomadic existence, eating and sleeping with any family that offered him shelter.

He led a nomadic existence, eating and sleeping with any family that offered him shelter.

Everybody knew him. He was very likeable and had no trouble finding families to stay with. But his life had no structure; he made his own plans and his own rules. He participated in our Saturday programs, and gradually, we built a relationship with him and became members of his very extended family.

At the camps we held annually, we were able to nurture our relationship with Mynor, and one day he opened his heart to us. When we held our evening campfire, Mynor was at the front of the group and began sharing about his life. He was crying, and slowly he opened up about the pain of his solitary life. Until then, only the Lord knew how Mynor had suffered.

After that camp, a very courageous member of our staff invited Mynor to live in her home. He enjoyed the soft bed, running water and good food for two days, but he could not survive within the structure of the family. He returned to the dump on foot, walking several miles to get to his "home."

For him, home wasn't even a place; it was the people who made him feel loved and comfortable. They were his family. We shared Jesus with him in words and deeds, but we did not see a change in the way he lived his life. He remained the cheerful vagabond everyone loved—right up until the night he died while sleeping on a pile of garbage. I don't know what killed him, but I hope to see him in heaven.

Why Waste My Time?

When they heard about people like Mynor, our friends would tell us that we were wasting our time. They said the Treasures were lazy and had no desire to change.

Sometimes I felt the same way. I told God, "Forget it. I can't keep this up." Especially when I saw a lot of suffering but no change, I felt like the man in the parable of the sower, whose seeds fell on rocky soil. Nevertheless, I was determined to be obedient to God—regardless of the results my human eyes saw.

> *I felt like the man in the parable of the sower, whose seeds fell on rocky soil.*

Why was I not born in a garbage dump? I don't have the answer to that question. I just know that I need to recognize God's love and mercy, even though I don't deserve them, without feeling guilty. I became more grateful for what God had given me. I had a family and a comfortable home; I was living in the lap of luxury in comparison with the scavengers I met every day.

In the garbage dump surrounded by dehumanizing circumstances I felt the eternal truth that made me want to share God's love in tangible ways—no matter how complicated or difficult it was.

Why did I not see their lives changed at that time? I don't know, but God knows and recognizes my obedience, which is enough for me.

> *And I, the King, will tell them, "When you did it*
> *to these my brothers, you were doing it to me!"–*
> **Matthew 25:40 (TLB)**

Personal or Group Follow-Up

Who would be considered the equivalent of Guatemala City's "scavengers" in your city? Why?

↪

According to Ephesians 2:10, where does the dignity of every human being come from?

↪

How do the labels that we attach to people either build up or tear down their divine dignity?

↪

How have you experienced guilt in the face of poverty?

↪

Have you ever felt as if you were not making a difference and wanted to quit? What kept you going?

CHAPTER 4

Understanding God's Heart for the Poor

"You sound like a communist."

"Isn't that the Social Gospel?"

"The work of Potter's House is great, but it's not God's work. God's work is planting churches."

Those were some of the arguments I heard from friends, relatives, pastors and visitors.

I was a psychologist, not a theologian. Was serving the poor something commanded by Jesus or merely a feel-good humanitarian endeavor promoted by a progressive culture? I wanted to be sure I knew the difference.

Other big questions I had centered on why there were people working in the garbage dump? The dump was created to dispose of garbage; why was God allowing His prize creation to depend on that garbage for their survival? What if I had been born into a scavenger family? Would I have been able to believe in a loving God? It seemed as if everything I learned about life in the garbage dump challenged my theology and my beliefs.

When Potter's House was born in 1986, Guatemala was still in the throes of a civil war that started in 1960 and didn't

Guatemala was still in the throes of a civil war that started in 1960 and didn't end until 1996.

end until 1996. The strife between the government of Guatemala and leftist rebel groups took place primarily in rural areas away from the capital city, but no one felt safe as tension swirled through our everyday lives.

And civil war was not the only thing that made us uneasy. Much of the rest of the world was engaged in the Cold War, and Central America—especially Guatemala, Cuba, El Salvador and Nicaragua—was a strategic target for both sides of that conflict.

The war caused the displacement of many people from rural areas. Fleeing violence and lack of jobs, they migrated to the capital city and ended up working in the garbage dump (which opened in 1954) as their only means of survival. The Civil War, which formally ended with the signing of a peace accord at the end of 1996, left Guatemala in turmoil. Seeking an end to the violence and corruption that had flourished during the war, Guatemalans were looking for a change in the political system.

The Politics of Change

The choice some of them saw was between the existing capitalist system and communism. Others turned to Liberation Theology, a Roman Catholic movement that arose in Latin America in the latter half of the 20th Century.

Liberation Theology held that the ministry of the Church must include involvement in civic and political affairs. It viewed as sinful the socio-economic structures that led to social and economic inequity and stressed the importance of the Christian's role in the struggle of the poor against the wealthy members of society. As it evolved, the movement's politics moved farther to the left, and it was eventually deemed Marxist by even the Roman Catholic Church.

While Liberation Theology was flourishing in Guatemala, I was studying at the University of San Carlos, the National University. Guatemala obviously had many problems, and this new movement presented solutions to many of them—especially the exploitation of minorities and the poor. It became part of the university culture to the extent that some said its proponents had been brain washed.

Some of my classmates, who believed that changing the political system was the way to change the country and the world, joined the movement. Some of them died in the pursuit of their convictions and dreams of a better Guatemala.

I remember one friend in particular. After the peace accord was signed and the civil war wound down, he seemed to forget that he was supposed to be defending the poor. I asked him whether he planned to continue fighting for the rights of the poor as his communist politics demanded. He shrugged his shoulders and answered, "I don't really care anymore. I have my career, a good job, a house, a car. I need to think about my own life now." His answer devastated me, because I knew he was one of the leaders who were recruiting other students to join the movement and die for the cause. The hypocrisy was staggering.

Civil war and the turmoil that followed taught us that political systems cannot change human beings.

Civil war and the turmoil that followed taught us that political systems cannot change human beings. We are selfish. We are sinners. And only Jesus can change us so we can help change our families, neighborhoods, and countries.

Participating in the movement of Christian College Students of Campus Crusade for Christ (now CRU) helped me understand the Christian view that change in a human being occurs from the inside out. Blaise Pascal said, "There is a God-shaped vacuum in the heart of every man which cannot be filled by any created thing, but only by God, the Creator made known through Jesus."

In John 7-37-38, Jesus said, *"Let anyone who is thirsty come to me and drink. Whoever believes in me, as Scripture has said, rivers of living water will flow from within them."*

As a student, I chose to believe those truths, but now, after more than 30 years of serving people living in poverty, I can tell you that they make a great deal more sense to me.

God alone changes a human life. As we read in Philippians 2:13, "...for it is God who works in you to will and to act in order to fulfill his good purpose."

Then Came the Earthquake

As if Guatemala had not suffered enough, on February 4, 1976, the country was shaken by an earthquake of magnitude 7.6 on the Richter Scale. About 25,000 people died, 77,000 were injured, countless buildings were destroyed.

It is essential to understand that the earthquake caused international organizations to come to Guatemala to serve the poor for the first time. Writing about that event, Dr. Virgilio Zapata, co-founder of the America Latina School and Ministries in Guatemala, reported the following. (Please note that the word "evangelical" as used in Guatemala is more accurately translated as "protestant" or "non-Catholic.")

"The Evangelical Church was unified in its response to this national tragedy, establishing through Alianza Evangelica an emergency committee (CEPA) that was recognized by the President of the Republic General Kjell Laugerud García and the international evangelical and secular community.

"Evangelical brothers and sisters from friendly countries, including the United States, Mexico, Singapore, and other Central American countries made significant cash and in-kind donations that which made it possible to rebuild thousands of homes, temporary shelters, churches and schools, as well as to provide food and medical aid to the thousands who lived in the third of the country that was damaged by the quake. At the same time, there was the genuine charity of the evangelicals, and it unified many churches that were together serving two million people they needed.

"Between 1882, when the first protestant missionary came to Guatemala, and 1976, the protestant population of Guatemala grew to only 7%. From 1976 to 2020, that population increased to 45%. What made the difference? Before the earthquake, the Gospel was preached in words as a doctrine. After the earthquake, the Gospel was shared in both words and deeds. What a significant impact the addition of those deeds had on our country!"

After the earthquake, the Gospel was shared in both words and deeds.

As part of the effort to help people who were in need after the earthquake, I went with a team from Campus Crusade to help our friends in Patzicia, an indigenous town in the highlands of Guatemala. It was the first time I had ministered to people living in poverty, but it did not inspire me to serve them. I still thought I was poor too.

Crisis of Faith

I grew up in an evangelical denomination with sound doctrine. I appreciate the Bible teachings I heard as a child, because they helped me grow in my journey with Christ. But when my Christian worldview collided with what I heard at the university and the suffering, injustice and fear that I saw in my country, I had a crisis of faith. What was the truth? Could Jesus really change the world? How could I reconcile the hardship I saw around me with my faith? I felt as if I were torn between two worlds—the world my church taught about and the hard reality of life in my country.

Greek Dualism, advocating the separation of my faith from the rest of my life, impacted my worldview as well. Dualism is the idea that all of life can be separated into two main categories, the sacred and the secular. This fragmented vision of reality puts "spiritual" things in the "sacred" category and "worldly" things in the "secular" category. The way in which we view our world and our faith shapes the way we live—the way we interact with God, man, and nature.

Dualism also leads to a hierarchy of callings. After all, doesn't it seem self-evident that some jobs are more holy than others? If you were to ask the average Christian, "What would be the highest calling in life?" he or she would probably answer, "to be a missionary." This valuing of "spiritual" callings over allegedly "non-spiritual" callings is the result of dualism. People who espoused dualism saw the ministry of Potter's House as primarily a social effort.

Then there was the holistic biblical worldview. In contrast to the dualistic view where God's sphere of influence is seen as limited to the spiritual and sacred, a holistic biblical worldview sees Christ as the Lord of all creation. As noted by Abraham

Kuyper, an influential theologian and prime minister of the Netherlands in the early 20th Century, "there is not a square inch in the whole domain of our human existence over which Christ who is Sovereign overall, does not cry, 'Mine!'"

A holistic worldview supports a single reality in which God is Lord over all. Everything is sacred. Everything is important. Everything has unity and coherence. There is no division between the spiritual and the material where one aspect is greater or more important than the other. A holistic biblical worldview begins with God, who created all things, and ends with God.

> A holistic worldview supports a single reality in which God is Lord over all.

Jesus came to restore all things. See Acts 3:21. The closer we walk with Jesus, the more we will be called to participate in the restoration of all things.

In 1986, ten years after the earthquake, I found myself serving the poor again, only this time the experience led me to a breakthrough in my Christian life. For the first time, I began to understand poverty in my country and especially among the Treasures who were living and working in the garbage dump. Because I felt called to serve them but I didn't know precisely how to do it, I began reading what the Bible says about serving the poor. I amassed 16 pages of Bible verses; I needed to know God's heart toward the poor.

As I became aware of the needs of my new friends and began to understand what God says about ministering to the poor, I started inviting others to serve with me. The answers of some of my friends were gratifying; they joined this small movement of God and got involved as volunteers and supporters of our fledgling ministry. Lisbeth and I understood we could not do it alone; there were many needs, and we wanted others to follow God's commandments.

But other friends reminded me of the way I had been in the past. They made excuses for not helping. They were not interested in serving the poor. They quoted Bible verses to support their views and their feelings. They quoted Jesus in John 12:8: "You will always have the poor among you, but you will not always have me."

Did Jesus Really Say That?

I was frustrated because I could not contradict a statement made by Jesus Himself, but I knew their interpretation was wrong. As I re-read that passage, I saw that it had been taken out of context. It was Jesus' reply to the disciples who criticized Mary for pouring expensive perfume on Jesus' feet and wiping them with her hair. In John 12:7, Jesus says, "Leave her alone. It was intended that she should save this perfume for the day of my burial."

I believe that what my friends were saying was that poverty is a big problem—too big for people like us to solve. It is an evil we must accept. Given that attitude, it was very difficult for me to find volunteers to help the Treasures, which made me both sad and angry. Then one day God told me, "Do not judge; you were the same. You didn't want to go to the garbage dump then any more than your friends do now."

I continued to study that verse and eventually understood that the statement about the poor was incomplete. In John 12:8, Jesus is quoting an important verse from the Old Testament— Deuteronomy 15:11: "There will always be poor people in the land. *Therefore, I command you* to be openhanded toward your brothers and the poor and needy in your land." In fact, that verse is the last of the 11 verses in that chapter that give the Israelites guidance in the ways they should handle money.

The reference is to the poor, afflicted, needy, weak, wretched person who is suffering from oppression and abuse—in general the lowest class in society then and now. My heart was released when I read the rest of the verse. I interpreted it as exercise in obedience to God and charity to my brothers and sisters who are in need.

> *The fact that there is poverty on the earth is not a judgment on humanity.*

In this verse, we can learn many lessons about the heart of God for the poor. First, serving the poor is not optional. The fact that there is poverty on the earth is not a judgment on humanity; it is an opportunity to serve and glorify God.

Second, the verse tells us that we should not harden our hearts. We should not keep our hand closed, holding on to our stuff. We should, instead, open that hand with a grateful heart—a heart thankful for what God has given us. And we should be generous in sharing our time, talents and treasure with our less-fortunate brothers and sisters, helping them to overcome their poverty. Deuteronomy 15:11 is merely the conclusion of the first ten verses of the chapter.

Being open-handed will not encourage the poor to depend on us. It is an opportunity to help them recognize our reliance on God, who is our Provider.

Why Do People Live in the Garbage Dump?

The civil war, the earthquake of 1976, the government corruption and other social problems in Guatemala created the chaos that led people to view the garbage dump as a desirable place to go.

Although I grew up in a Christian home, went to church, and had many opportunities to participate in Christian groups, I never learned how to minister to poor people.

I realized that I was living a comfortable, average Christian life. I needed to soften my hard heart and become generous to people beyond the four walls of the church. I needed to start expressing God's love in tangible ways.

Serving God's people is God's work. He calls his children to be openhanded toward the poor and needy!

> *"He defended the cause of the poor and needy,*
> *and so all went well.*
> *Is that not what it means to know me?"*
> *declares the Lord.—***Jeremiah 22:16**

Personal or Group Follow-Up

What is your theological basis for caring for the poor?

⟿

What are the cultural factors that have contributed to poverty in your culture?

⟿

In practical terms, what does a holistic Biblical worldview mean to you and your organization? Why is this important?

⟿

What are some formative experiences and principles that God has used to teach you about ministering to poor people?

Additional Resources

Holy Discontent: Fueling the Fire that Ignites Personal Vision.
   Bill Hybels. Zondervan. 2007

The Body: Being Light in Darkness, Charles Colson and Ellen Santilli
   Vaughn. Word Publishing.1992.

CHAPTER 5

A Favor Becomes A Calling

The ministry was flourishing. Lisbeth and I continued to work in the Christian counseling center, using our offices there as our headquarters, and going to the garbage dump on weekends and whenever we were needed there.

In the beginning, we held Bible Clubs for children in the church that helped us to deliver the blankets that first Christmas Eve. But we outgrew that space when children started bringing their siblings and friends, so we rented the facilities of a Christian school near the dump. The added space allowed us to serve more children, and we were able to add clubs for teens and mothers along with a small medical clinic.

When one of our supporters suggested that we purchase property near the dump, I reacted badly. I knew what my calling was; I was happy and comfortable in my counseling ministry. I counseled my own clients and taught pastors how to counsel their flocks. I did not have time for another major commitment, so I dragged my feet, embarking on the property search without enthusiasm.

I learned, to my relief, that real estate prices around the garbage dump were surprisingly high. I was sure we would never be able to afford to buy land.

Bargaining with God

While we looked for property, I prayed, trying to convince the Lord that I knew what was best for my life. Having grown up in Guatemala, where almost anything can be bought for a better price, I was a skillful bargainer. So I bargained with God. I said, "You know, Lord, there are not enough Christian counselors in my country. You led me to this profession, and I studied for six years to be able to counsel and help Your people." In my heart, I wanted to continue to serve the poor from my comfortable office. I reminded God that I was already going to the dump on my day off. What more could He want?

In my heart, I wanted to continue to serve the poor from my comfortable office.

Then we found the property! That was my first clue that my life was no longer my own. Despite my pleas, God had given us a piece of land. So I stopped trying to persuade Him that I knew best and surrendered to Him. "God," I prayed, "You know I don't want to work in that dump. This is not part of my plan. I am afraid to go there, but if You give me peace and the conviction that this is Your will, I will follow You."

As soon as I made that commitment, I realized that my human goals and aspirations were limited and temporary, but when I surrendered my life completely to God, little-by-little His vision became mine. His love for the poor became like a fire kindled in my heart. My life was no longer about me; it was about God's plans and His Kingdom.

As I look back on that time, I realize that my God was way too small. I simply could not imagine a better life of service than the one I was living. But God had more for me—much more.

In February 1993, after finding the property and coming to believe that the Lord was calling us to serve His Treasures full-time, we started the process of becoming a legal nonprofit organization in Guatemala. With the blessing of the first board of directors, Lisbeth and I, gave birth to *Asociación Casa del Alfarero*—Potter's House Association (PHA).

We had the calling; we had the vision. Now all we needed was direction. So we focused on listening—hearing God's voice—as we moved ahead.

Location, Location, Location

Our new property was located about 50 feet from the cliff that marked the edge of the dump. The only building on it was a small adobe building near the street. There was no running water. There was no telephone (and no one had a cell phone back then). There was no bathroom, only a filthy outhouse in the middle of the property. Dirty water flooded the area when it rained. The only plants were scraggly weeds, and it was home to a pig and swarms of flies. The pig belonged to a neighbor, but the flies seemed to belong to us.

The pig belonged to a neighbor, but the flies seemed to belong to us.

The unpaved street in front of the clinic was often clogged with derelict cars and giant bags of recyclables that people had collected from the dump. Our neighbors lived in small shacks made of corrugated tin like most of the other Treasures. When we needed water, we got it from one of the shared faucets scattered around the area.

The first doctors, Lucky Hernandez, a Guatemalan friend, and Steve Hammer, an American missionary, moved our medical clinic from the church to our new building.

Dr. Steve remembers, "We started by stapling plastic to the rotted ceiling so that debris like termite dust would not fall on our patients. Consultations began before we even put up a sign; there was no need for advertising.

"The clinic was furnished with very simple wooden tables and chairs. When we arrived in the morning, we would sweep the flies that had died overnight from our desks. The acrid smell of burning garbage from the dump was inescapable. There was no telephone line, but we did have electricity. After 18 months we acquired a hose, but we still had no sink or bathroom.

"We used baby wipes to clean our hands. Any patient whose care required cleaner conditions was sent to a small Christian hospital."

We charged the equivalent of only a few U.S. cents for a consultation, but we never turned anyone away for lack of money. We believed that charging at least a token amount was good for two reasons: It allowed patients to maintain their dignity, and it made it clear to them that what they were receiving was of value.

Gradually, we were able to get exam tables and more equipment. We showed Christian videos in the cramped waiting room to entertain patients while they waited their turn. The kids, especially, liked videos about David Wilkerson and Nicky Cruz's ministry, possibly because they could relate to the violence and gang life portrayed in them.

Jerry and Barbara Murphy also did a lot of work with the clinic during that time. Jerry was a pharmacist, and he and Barbara trained young Guatemalans Douglas de la Cruz and Magda Batz to work as pharmacists, dispensing donated medications to our clinic patients.

Phase Two: Education

Once the medical clinic was up and running in our new facility, we turned to the children of the scavengers and launched the Kids' Bible Program, which drew many enthusiastic little ones who couldn't wait to check out the new neighbors on the block.

The Lord provided Guatemalan volunteers whom we trained to help us serve those Little Treasures. We divided them into small groups and sat them on concrete blocks because we had no chairs or tables.

The Kids' Bible Program was obviously meeting a need. It grew and grew, so we added more small groups. The children were thrilled to have a place to go every week. They received a lot of love from the volunteers, participated in activities designed especially for them, and of course, enjoyed a delicious snack, all the while learning about Jesus and the Bible.

Our next step was to open a trade school where Treasures could learn skills like a masonry and carpentry. For the mothers, we offered sewing classes. The trade school was not a great success, but we learned a great deal from it. We learned that to be successful the Treasures needed a level of structure that was

> *We learned that to be successful the Treasures needed a level of structure that was not part of their culture.*

41

not part of their culture. We also learned that most of them were illiterate. As we thought about ways to address those two issues, God led us to create the Potter's House Education Program, which is still going strong today.

In the beginning, we had to beg the parents to allow their children to participate in the program. Volunteers Yasmina Garcia and Miriam Aquino went out into the dump community to recruit kids for the new program. Then they worked on the program itself, designing a curriculum and creating a structure that would help the children do well in school.

What a celebration we had when the first class finished Kindergarten! We grew the program year-by-year, adding a grade each year until we had a class of 6th graders who graduated from elementary school. We had a big event at the end of that school year, providing inspiration for the entire community and raising awareness of the importance of education.

The parents were very proud of their kids' accomplishments, even though they themselves had made little use of what education they had received. They and their parents knew that the boys were destined to become scavengers in the dump where education was not required. It was an even bigger waste of time for girls, who needed to care for younger siblings at home until they themselves became mothers. Once a girl left her parents' home and moved in with her husband's family, she was at the mercy of her mother-in-law, whose bidding she would do for decades to come. Education might make her less willing to accept that scenario.

With that as a background, many parents decided to send their children to our school. They realized that education would probably have made their own lives easier, and they wanted their kids to take advantage of the opportunities God was offering them through Potter's House.

The first of our Treasures to graduate from college was Magda Batz, who went on to receive a master's degree in social work. Since then, the Potter's House Education Program has grown and improved a great deal. The majority of our students finish 6ᵗʰ grade, and we now see about 20 students graduating from private high schools every year. Of those, more and more are going on to attend and graduate from university.

By His grace, God has given me the opportunity to travel to the United States and attend the graduations of two of the five Treasures who attended universities in the United States through the Walton International Scholarship Fund. As I sat at those graduations, I praised the Lord. It was nothing short of a miracle; my human mind never suspected that doing a favor so many years earlier would lead to that place of joy and fulfillment.

> *God has given me the opportunity to travel to the United States and attend the graduations of two of the five Treasures who attended universities in the United States*

God called Lisbeth and me to a task that seemed mundane to us, when, in fact, His perfect plan was to involve us in a miracle. We did an ordinary, everyday thing when we shared the blankets that first Christmas Eve. He did a miracle, using those blankets as the foundation for a ministry that has lasted for more than 34 years.

Only God can touch lives and give life. When God asks you to do something you think is mundane and perhaps not even worth your time, I urge you to do it anyway—with all your heart. I try to have that attitude toward anything that looks ordinary to me, but it's not always easy. God wants us to move forward on the Christian-growth continuum, trusting in a

Faithful One every step of the way—no matter how mundane or ordinary the steps may seem.

What would have happened if I had not agreed to deliver those blankets? Of course, God could have used someone else to get the job done, but I would have missed the blessing of being part of the miracles He has done in the lives of His Treasures. Thank you, Lord, for calling me!

You did not choose me, but I chose you and appointed you that you should go and bear fruit and that your fruit should abide, so that whatever you ask the Father in my name, he may give it to you.—**John 15:16 (ESV)**

Personal or Group Follow-Up

In what ways have you tried to "bargain" with God regarding His calling in your life?

↝

How has your view of God been too small?

↝

The co-founders of Potter's House started by taking small steps. What were some of the small steps you have taken or plan to take to address poverty?

↝

What does it mean for you to be obedient to God's leading even in the mundane things? What are some of those mundane things for you, and how might God have a bigger plan at work?

CHAPTER 6

Praying for Men

When the Lord called us to serve Him in the garbage dump, many of our friends thought that Lisbeth and I, two single young women, were crazy. They thought we were wasting our education and the ability to earn money as psychologists. They predicted that we would soon lose interest in this questionable project.

But we did it anyway. Even though our small, inexperienced, all-woman staff had a lot to learn, we persevered. We knew nothing about running an organization and very little about serving the poor. What we did know how to do was share God's love and His word. I believe that in those early days God planted in our hearts the seed that became a passion. Potter's House was His idea from the start.

At the same time, as the ministry was growing, I was dealing with the pressure of being single. I was 33-years old, and my friends did not hesitate to offer advice. They wanted to know what had happened to me, why I was so picky. They suggested that my standards for a husband were too high.

One of them summed it up by asking, "Are you sure you want to serve there? You know you will never get married; who in the world is going to find you in that place?" She assured me that my chances of finding the

I continued to pray for the husband God had for me, but I didn't get any answers.

husband I longed for would be all but nonexistent if I continued on this path. Her assertion and the questions and accusations of others made me feel as if my singleness was my fault. I began to believe that there was something wrong with me; I was ugly and didn't deserve to get married. I continued to pray for the husband God had for me, but I didn't get any answers.

Back when we started working in the dangerous dump community, I had prayed, "Lord, please protect me in this environment; make me unattractive to the men in this community." Years later, I told God, "You seem to have taken my prayer seriously, because not a single man has paid any attention to me since I started working here."

Despite the challenges of being single in a family-oriented culture, I began to understand that God had made me for something and for someone. I decided to focus all my energy and flexible time on serving Him and the children I had come to love. I saw myself as a pioneer—a pioneer surrounded by challenges and suffering. My new friends were suffering in extreme poverty, and I lacked the experience necessary to help and serve them.

Sometimes I felt God had given me the gift of celibacy so I could concentrate on His work, and eventually I gave up the idea of marriage. My prayer was "If God wants me to be single, I want to be a happy, joyful single old lady."

Lord, Send Us Men

Initially, only women were interested in working at PHA. My friend was right; it was going to be difficult to attract men to the ministry. But we felt that we needed male staff members to minister to the men and teenage boys who were coming for the Bible studies. In addition, some of the men from the community started asking us to create programs for them like the ones we had for women and children. So, once again, I began to pray—this time that God would send men—not for me but for our staff.

The Lord answered our prayer in the person of Héctor Rivas. He knew the ministry well, because he had started serving as a volunteer in 1987 when he was 11-years old. We knew him well, too—his love for the kids, his calling to serve God, and his dedication to our work—so when he graduated from high school in November 1993, we asked him to join the staff. He must have enjoyed the job, because he went on to become the executive director of Potter's House.

Having Héctor on our team confirmed that we really needed men to help us serve the Treasures, so Lisbeth and I continued praying and inviting men to join to the staff.

In 1993, I was recruiting short-term volunteers for a children's camp. At the same time, a friend invited me to her birthday party and introduced me to a young man named Edgar Güitz. He was working with Youth for Christ at the time, and I thought that his love for kids would make him an excellent volunteer. I explained the opportunity to him, and he agreed to help. He was also a prayer warrior who came faithfully to Potter's House to pray with Lisbeth and me every Thursday.

Edgar, who had his own business and knew a lot about running a successful organization, told us how impressed he was by the team of brave, competent women who were running Potter's House. At the same time, he wondered where the men were. Lisbeth and I

Lisbeth and I prayed that God would work in Edgar's heart and call him to serve the poor in his own city.

prayed that God would work in Edgar's heart and call him to serve the poor in his own city.

We finally decided that the time was right to invite Edgar to be part of our staff. What we didn't know was that he was interested in full-time ministry and had told God that he would say "yes" to the first ministry that made him an offer. Guess who arrived the next day to ask him to consider joining our staff—Lisbeth and Gladys! He accepted our offer with the promise of a five-year commitment starting in January of 1994.

In addition to his passion for prayer, Edgar had been entrusted by God with the gifts of administration and vision. With God's help, he brought some sorely needed order to the ministry's accounting. Neither Lisbeth nor I even knew how to read a balance sheet, so his skills were much appreciated.

God had blessed us with Héctor Rivas and Edgar Güitz, two very capable men whose talents and vision for the ministry reinforced and improved much of what we were doing. We were finally free to focus more on the relationships we were building with the Treasures.

As I got to know him better, I appreciated Edgar's ideas and spiritual insights even more. We worked together well and soon became good friends.

A Husband for Auntie Gladys

It was about that time that my young nephew Javier began praying for a husband for his Auntie Gladys. His prayer request was for "a man who loves God, who loves Auntie Gladys and who loves the kids in the garbage dump."

Edgar was the answer to that prayer. But the first time he proposed to me, I changed the subject, because I was embarrassed.

I was quite a bit older than he, and I couldn't believe he was serious. I tried to banish the thought from my mind, telling myself it was not possible. But that day, my heart changed, and I began to realize that I was in love with him. He had something that the older men I knew didn't have, and even though he was young, he was much more mature than most of them.

I was careful not to show my feelings; I didn't want him to know that I was in love with him. I couldn't shake the shame I felt because he was so much younger than I. Then one day, he invited me out to dinner and used that time to clarify his feelings for me. He knew, he said, that he was taking a big risk; I would either say "yes," or he would lose a good friend. The night before that dinner, I prayed, asking God to help me understand what was happening in my heart. Only He and my sister (Javier's mom) knew what was going on in my heart.

Edgar said that he had a list of the qualities he wanted in a wife. As he got to know me, he started checking off items on the list and adding other traits I had that he never realized he wanted. That night over dinner, he opened his heart and shared his love for me. I responded by asking a lot of serious questions; I wanted to be very sure that he was really in love with me. Finally, I took a deep breath and confessed that I was feeling the same way. Poor Edgar. I had been reluctant to share my love with him because I was worried about what others would think. That night he said he slept well; I couldn't sleep at all.

Poor Edgar. I had been reluctant to share my love with him because I was worried about what others would think.

That was the beginning of our love story. It was not easy, especially for me, because I was a people pleaser, and I found myself focusing on what I thought others were saying about our relationship rather than what pleased God.

Another disappointment I faced was that I had had a hysterectomy as a treatment for uterine tumors. Edgar, who loved children, knew that I could not have them, and he loved me anyway—just the way I was.

I was still conflicted, wishing that I could be like other women—women who married young, had children, and enjoyed beautiful families. I shared with my dad what was happening in my life—that Edgar had proposed to me and that I was having reservations because I was older and could not have children. Down deep, I think I was hoping that my dad would tell me not to marry this man, but he said, "Daughter, this is the man that I have been praying for for you."

Still not convinced, I decided to release Edgar from his proposal, but before I had a chance to talk to him about it, he gave me a letter he had written describing how God was confirming his decision. Edgar then encouraged me to ask God for a message from His word.

Together, we prayed, and the Lord gave us Psalm 20. We now read this Psalm every anniversary and praise Him for the gift of our marriage.

With the blessing of our parents, we decided to get married on my birthday, August 24, 1996. Before God and 2,000 witnesses we promised to be faithful and join our lives for His kingdom. We invited Treasures from the community who had never attended a church wedding before. They were impressed with the solemnity and the joy of the occasion, and afterwards some of the couples who had been living together without being married decided to set things right and get married themselves.

Two special things happened during our courtship. One was that I introduced my nephew Javier to Edgar. I said, "Javier, would you please tell Edgar about your prayer request?" He did so, and I used that moment to tell Javier that this man, Edgar, was the answer to his prayer. Javier responded by hugging him and exclaiming, "my Uncle!" As people heard about Javier's prayer, some of our friends who were single asked my sister if Javier could pray for them.

Another special thing we did was to invite Cristobal, a Treasure who came from a family of alcoholics, to celebrate Christmas with my family. While he was there, we told him that we were going to get married. Cristobal expressed his happiness for us and then took Edgar aside and whispered, "please promise me that you will never beat her—ever." His request touched us both, and after 20 years of marriage, we happened to meet him on one of our visits to the garbage dump community. I asked if he remembered what he had said to Edgar that Christmas so long ago. He said that he did, so I told him that Edgar had never beaten me—ever. He just smiled.

The Lord in His mercy provided a husband to whom I have been married for 24 years. The Lord called him to the next level of service when he became the executive director of Potter's House. Then in 2016 when he was 50-years old, Edgar felt his mission had been accomplished at PHA. God called him to share with other ministries all that he had learned during of 25 years of serving the Lord at Potter's House.

Serving Together

I have enjoyed serving together with my love and my partner. I could never have imagined the joy and blessing that come with serving the Lord together as a couple.

> *I could never have imagined the joy and blessing that come with serving the Lord together as a couple.*

We never had children of our own, but God has allowed us to love and serve many kids who needed parents. Although the Lord was healing my heart as I faced infertility, there were some difficult times. One of the most challenging was picking up new mothers and their babies at the national hospital, because there was no one else to take them home. I asked God why I had to be the one to do such a painful thing, and eventually he answered with this thought: "Gladys, you and Edgar are an example of love as a couple. Love for each other does not require that you have children." That was a special revelation to me, coming as I do from a culture in which women think children are the anchors that keep their husbands from straying. They think that their value lies in the children they produce, and the more children they have, the more valuable they feel. God has, indeed, been merciful to me and given me His favor.

I used to ask to myself what would have happened if I had continued focusing on the opinion of my friends rather than following God's calling. Fortunately, I realized in time that it is more important to please God than to please others. Sometimes following God makes others think we are crazy and wasting our time.

The Lord answered many of our prayers as we started serving the Treasures. Little did I know that my future husband would be one of them!

Ask the Lord of the harvest, therefore,
to send out workers into his harvest field.
—Matthew 9:38

Personal or Group Follow-Up

What pressures regarding singleness or married life have you felt from the expectations of others?

⌐⊃

How do your attitudes towards singleness or married life impact those around you? Do they reflect God's heart?

⌐⊃

Who has God sent into your life to help fulfill His calling in you? How so?

⌐⊃

In what ways have you shared the special events in your life with those in your community of ministry?

⌐⊃

How have you allowed the opinion of your friends to influence you more than the calling of God?

CHAPTER 7

From Trash to Treasure

When we first started serving the dump community, we relied on gifts-in-kind to bless our new friends. Clothing, beans, rice, cereal, shampoo, shoes, fruit, vegetables—we never knew exactly what the Lord would provide, but we knew He knew our needs. We continued to trust Him to help us help the scavengers.

One morning, we received word that there was a donation of clothing awaiting pickup. It was my turn to retrieve the donation, so I headed out, eager to see what the Lord had for us. But when I arrived at the donor's home, I was shocked to see that the clothes being donated were dirty, stained and musty. Of course, I thanked the lady and put the bags in my truck. But I was angry. I wanted to tell her, "I can't take these; the scavengers will never use them," but Guatemalans are very polite, so I resisted the temptation and drove off.

Why had God allowed me to use precious time and gasoline to pick up a useless and insulting gift?

On my way back to Potter's House, I had an angry conversation with myself and with the Lord. What made that woman think that my friends would wear such awful clothes? Why did I thank her when her donation was not good enough for God's people? Why had God allowed me to use precious time and gasoline to pick up a useless and insulting gift?

57

I focused on the insult and the waste of resources, but the Lord used the situation to teach me that many people, like this donor, felt that the scavengers were worthy of only garbage and scraps—things wealthier people found disgusting. When I returned to Potter's House, I threw the donations into the dump.

My heart was heavy, I felt sad, and my soul was troubled; I didn't understand what had just happened. My new friends, who had started to become part of my family, were being treated like trash. People saw them as less than human. Yet I knew that God loved them and gave them the right to be treated as His beloved children, even though they were living in terrible circumstances.

Through that one donation, God taught me that He never intended His prize creation to live in a dump. The scavengers are human beings made, like all of us, in the image of God. Society scorns them, but they have courage and dignity. They work very hard. Many love their families just as much as we love ours, and many of them know the Lord and rely on Him in the midst of their suffering.

When I shared my clothing donation experience with some friends who were supporting the ministry, they sympathized and began to help us think of ways to better communicate the humanity of the people who lived in the dump community. They suggested that we stop calling our new friends "scavengers"— a word that has a distinctly negative connotation. But what could we call them? We thought and prayed about it until one day the Lord revealed the name "Treasures." He reminded us that they are Treasures because they are created in His image and carry that image no matter where they live, no matter where they work, no matter what their rank on the socio-economic ladder.

So we started calling them "Treasures," and the name stuck. Today Potter's House serves Treasures not just in the Guatemala City garbage dump community but in other impoverished areas of the country as well.

Little Treasures

Children born into the dump community have the odds stacked against them from the start. Surrounded by poverty, they are very vulnerable; yet they are the ones whose futures can be changed.

When they are very young, most of them are unaware that they live in a culture of poverty—a culture that robs them of the ability to dream of a better life. When they begin to realize that they are surrounded by hardship, they have no idea that they have the power to change their destinies through hard work and perseverance.

At Potter's House, we firmly believe that education is the key to a better future for children. But for parents struggling every day, it can be difficult to prioritize education when a child in school is a child who cannot help support the family. Often, the children themselves feel it is their duty to start working when they complete the compulsory portion of their education at the end of 6th grade.

Other children battle learning disabilities brought on by malnutrition and poor medical care, finding it difficult to succeed in school, while still others simply lack the discipline needed to stay in school. With no encouragement from their parents, they abandon their educations as soon as they can legally do so.

From the very beginning, Potter's House has worked hard to teach parents the importance of educating their children. Initially, they resisted our efforts, but with much perseverance and the Lord's guidance, we were able to change their hearts

> *From the very beginning, Potter's House has worked hard to teach parents the importance of educating their children.*

and help them recognize the value of education. Our vision of educating children grew, and we thrived. Eventually, we established an after-school tutoring program to help our Little Treasures succeed in school.

According to the Guatemala Ministry of Education, only 43% of secondary school-aged students enroll in school for the equivalent of grades 7 to 9. Only 24% continue to study in grades 10 to 12. These are the worst statistics in Latin America, which has an average secondary school enrollment rate of 69%.

One reason for those abysmal numbers is that the public secondary schools in Guatemala not only offer a very poor quality of education but are hotbeds of drug use and gang activity. That means that private schools are the only option for students who want to receive a quality education in a secure environment.

Private schools in Guatemala, although usually less expensive than private schools in other countries, are far from free. Even parents in the dump community who understand the value of education are unable to afford it for their older children. By the time our Little Treasures were old enough to enter 7th grade, we had found some generous donors who aided us by providing financial support for the few children who wanted to continue their studies in secondary school. At that point, college was merely a pipe dream.

As we began to understand more about poverty, the PHA staff realized that breaking the cycle of poverty required a holistic approach. As we built our program, we strove to ensure that we were helping the children and their families grow in all areas of their lives—body, mind, and spirit.

We praise the Lord continuously as every year more children decide to continue their education. This is a great achievement and, at the same time, a great challenge as we work to provide the academic and spiritual support they need and raise the funds for private school tuition.

God has provided, and hundreds of Treasures have finished high school. Some have graduated from university, and some are still completing their university studies. Their rewards are jobs outside the garbage dump and the financial wherewithal to help their families live better lives.

A Treasure's Story

Kathy Rosales is a Treasure who took full advantage of everything the Lord offered her through Potter's House. She joined our program when she was 4-years old. When she was 8, her father was killed, and her mother, Lorena, was left alone to provide for her five children.

Lorena herself had no education, so her only way of making a living was to work in the garbage dump. But she suffers from a congenital hip malformation that put her at a disadvantage in competing with other Treasures scrambling to find the best garbage in the dump. So her two oldest children (9- and 14-years old at the time) dropped out of school to help her scavenge. Kathy feared that the same fate awaited her.

Potter's House provided the hope that saved her. Because she was committed to attending our after-school tutoring program, she never had to work in the garbage dump. Another welcome benefit was that her mom did not have to worry about her lunch because Potter's House served a nutritious lunch every school day to her and her younger siblings. In addition, she found loving support that helped her concentrate on her studies and envision a better and brighter future for herself, her family, and even her community.

She found loving support that helped her concentrate on her studies and envision a better and brighter future for herself, her family, and even her community.

On November 30, 2012, Kathy graduated from a private high school with a diploma that qualified her to work as a bilingual secretary in Guatemala. One reason she chose that career path was that she was determined to learn English so she could communicate with her Potter's House sponsors, whom she calls her American grandparents.

In 2006, the Lord had opened a door for the Treasures through the Walton International Scholarship Program. This generous program provides full scholarships to qualified students from Central America to obtain undergraduate degrees from one of several universities in

Arkansas. Kathy was one of five Treasures accepted into the program between 2006 and 2012; she graduated from Harding University in 2017 with a bachelor's degree in marketing and international business.

Kathy has become a beautiful young woman. She married her husband, Selvin, in 2018 and is currently working in another ministry that serves the poor. She is an example of what the

Bible says in Psalm 113:8, "He lifts the poor from the dust and the needy from the garbage dump. He sets them among princes, even the princes of his own people!" (NLT) Kathy is a princess among her own people and an example of what an early Potter's House newsletter meant when it declared: "Let not where we were born dictate how we will live."

Personal or Group Follow-up

What's wrong with giving away your used stuff to someone who might still find value in it?

How does what we believe about people affect the way that we talk about them? How does the way we talk about people affect what they believe about themselves?

Why is it important to think holistically about family structures in breaking the cycle of generational poverty?

CHAPTER 8

A Lingering Joy

"Agua! Agua!" the children cried out when they arrived at our first camp and saw a quiet waterfall.

Imagine all the things they were seeing for the first time. Everything was green, there was water, there were flowers, and there were rooms with bunk beds—one for each of them. At home, most of them slept on the floor or with several other kids and/or adults on a single mattress. At the camp, God also provided blankets, sheets, towels, clothes, shampoo, and soap.

With a small team of volunteers, including my dad, we embarked upon our grand adventure. We couldn't wait to take the children and teenagers out of the garbage dump. For many of them, it was their first time on a bus.

Since the beginning, God reminded us to do our best because we were doing it for Him.

For many of the children it was their first trip away from their families and the garbage dump community. Some of them told us that they had packed their suitcases (garbage bags) the week before with the best clothes they had. Others were so excited that they could not sleep the night before.

Because food was scarce in the dump community, the children viewed the simple camp meals as a bountiful banquet. Some of them decided not to eat all of their food, storing it in their pockets in case there was no dinner. We were able to tell them that God had provided three meals for each of the four days of camp. They could not believe it.

So Much Water!

The first night, we noticed that the kids did not want to go to bed. They were having too much fun playing in the bathroom, taking showers and reveling in the limitless supply of water. At home, most of them would bathe by ladling water from a barrel. Their mothers would wake up early in the morning to join the line of people waiting for water with which to fill that barrel. Water was available only sporadically, so most of them were unable to bathe daily.

At home, most of them would bathe by ladling water from a barrel.

Swimming was a new and exciting pleasure for the children, as well. One day we even did the Bible lesson in the water.

A surprise outing was included in the camp program, and the children were delighted. One destination was a safari park. Floridalma, one of the kids on the bus that day, recalls, "the animals were loose and came toward us. An ostrich stuck his head inside our bus!"

Their parents could never have afforded a field trip like this, so this adventure was beyond a child's wildest dreams. God was good!

"I remember that once we came back from seeing all the wild animals, there was an activity in which we designed a t-shirt. With paint, we drew animals on the shirts," says Floridalma, who is now 37-years old. Like Floridalma, the children enjoyed this unique activity and continue to reminiscence about it years later.

Camp bonfires provided a peaceful atmosphere where children listened closely to God's Word, reflecting on their different devotional times throughout the day.

"Many children invited Jesus into their hearts that night. It was something special," says Floridalma.

That first kids' camp at Potter's House was a milestone because parents trusted the ministry enough to let their children go with us. Establishing trust was and is an essential element in effectively serving the dump community where trust is a precious and scarce commodity.

Establishing trust was and is an essential element in effectively serving the dump community where trust is a precious and scarce commodity.

It required a step of faith for parents to allow their kids to go with us—even for a couple days. They had to trust us to take care of their children and bring them back safe and sound. After the first camp, which was for boys, we decided to do a second one for girls. We invited some of the mothers to go along, to give them an opportunity to spend precious time with their daughters. They loved the experience so much, that we later invited a group of mothers to enjoy a one-day field trip to the country. Most of them had become mothers at such a young age that they never had a chance to have the kind of fun their kids were having with us.

Were We Hurting Them?

When donors and volunteers heard about the camp, some of them disapproved. "It must have been a shock for them to come home to the dump after being at camp," they said. "We think you might be hurting them instead of helping them by taking them to beautiful places and showing them things they would never otherwise see." I was very disappointed in their response, but as always, their questions helped us to think about what we were doing. We wondered whether we were, in fact, hurting them.

But none of the children appeared to experience any negative effects, so we decided to continue the program. We saw that it was good for them to learn how to function in a new environment and participate in new activities—especially the times we had to talk with them about God. So whenever God provided the opportunity, we would take a group of kids to camp for a day or two.

As we pondered the negative response of some of our friends, a verse from James 1:7 came to us: "Every good thing is given and every perfect gift is from above, coming down from the Father of lights with whom there is no variation or shifting shadow. (NASB) Then we knew that we were giving them opportunities to experience joy and happiness that only God could provide. Every good gift we shared with them was from Him.

Personal or Group Follow-Up

In practical terms, what does it mean for you to "do your best" because you are doing it for God?

↭

What are things that you do intentionally to build trust with the people you serve? What could you do better?

↭

Does exposing the poor to experiences outside of their normal reach cause them to feel overwhelmed or to dream big?

CHAPTER 9

Beginning to Understand Poverty (Part One)

"Problem? The garbage dump is not a problem; it is a blessing! This is where I find food and things that I recycle and sell to support my family."

That was the answer of a lady we asked, "What do you think about the problem of the garbage?" That response confirmed to us that there was still a great deal we did not know about poverty.

After almost ten years of serving the poor, the Potter's House staff began to wonder exactly how much we really knew about poverty. Our years of service had taught us a lot, but we felt that there was much more to learn.

So in 1995, in an effort to deepen our understanding of poverty, the staff went door-to-door, interviewing residents of the community surrounding the garbage dump and asking questions like the one above.

Around the same time, the Municipality of Guatemala City launched a project that provided sturdy concrete-block homes for some of the Treasures. Those homes were a gift from the Lord to those who received them. Instead of living in decrepit shacks, families had real houses. It was very exciting! The Treasures participated in the project, guarding the materials at night so no one would steal them and helping with construction during the day.

When the day arrived for a family to take possession of a finished home, we celebrated with them as they received the keys to their front door. It was a joyful fiesta, and we loved seeing them about to start a new life in a clean, new environment.

Each house had two private bedrooms, a small dining room with a kitchen, a complete bathroom, and an outdoor space or patio with a sink. But when we visited them in their new homes a few months later, we found that the Treasures were not using the houses as intended. Instead, they used them as storage for all the things they collected in the dump. For them, garbage was not a problem; it was a valuable thing that deserved as much care as—sometimes more than—the members of the family. We called it the "garbage mentality."

New donors and people who were just learning about our work often asked, "How many people have you helped move out of the dump community?" How could we reply? We still didn't completely understand the problem, and our friends thought they had an easy answer. What we had realized by then was that our goal was not to remove the Treasures from the garbage but to remove the garbage from their minds.

In the beginning, those questions upset me, but as time went on, I learned that the seemingly naïve questions of our friends were helping us to dig deeper as we sought to understand our Treasures and their environment.

The first thing you see when dealing with poverty is the obvious economic poverty. That is how most people define poverty, but we found that lack of resources is superficial. Addressing only economic poverty is like grabbing an animal by its tail; it will eventually turn on you and bite the hand that is feeding it.

Fortunately, Potter's House did not have a great many economic resources to apply to the poverty that surrounded us, so we were forced to focus on other needs. In addition to learning by observation, we undertook a systematic evaluation of the community's needs, through which the Lord revealed what we call the Eight Forms of Poverty.

The Eight Forms of Poverty have become the backbone of our approach to fighting poverty, providing the structure that we use to create strategies for holistic ministry that equips the Treasures to overcome their circumstances.

The first five forms of poverty have to do with the individual person—body, mind and spirit. The other three focus on relationships with others. Let's take a look at the first three forms of poverty and the scriptures that led us to them.

1. Spiritual Poverty

> *Blessed are the poor in Spirit for theirs is*
> *the kingdom of Heaven.*—**Matthew 5:3**

Defined as *Christian Life versus Religiosity,* Spiritual Poverty is not a lack of religion but a lack of a relationship with God—the living God who made us, who knows us intimately, and wants to enter into a loving relationship with us.

Many members of the dump community are religious. They go to church regularly but lack a personal relationship with God to sustain them. Bianca Pu was one such Treasure.

While growing up, Bianca felt a void in her heart and searched high and low for something to fill it. "I used to go to bars with my friends every night of the week and leave my children at home. I would drink every night, and I loved to smoke. I didn't care that I was hurting my children and my husband. I eventually started sniffing cocaine in the bathroom so my children wouldn't see me. On Saturday nights and Sunday mornings,

I would go to church and pretend to praise God. I was even part of the praise and worship team, but my heart was elsewhere."

Bianca realized that her life was upside-down and asked God to help her turn her life around. She found herself at the feet of Christ and gave her life to Him. As she focused on Him and started to participate in a discipleship group at Potter's House, her life changed. "I liked going to my discipleship group because I learned how to be a good neighbor and mother. I also learned how to pray," she remembers.

> *Bianca realized that her life was upside-down and asked God to help her turn her life around.*

Ricardo, the man with whom Bianca had been living, came to our program as a child and participated in the trade school that we had for a while. After Bianca started living for Christ, her relationship with Ricardo was restored, and they decided to honor God's word and get married. They understood that Jesus offers life in all its fullness: The thief comes only to steal and kill and destroy; I have come that they may have life, and have it to the full. John 10:10

With joy in her heart, Bianca participated in a jewelry-making class at Potter's House, and when she discovered that she had a talent for making jewelry, she started a small business selling the necklaces, earrings, and bracelets that she designed and made. Ricardo did not return to the garbage dump, where he had been working, and began to help her with the business. They also taught other women how to execute Bianca's designs and bought the jewelry they made.

When Ricardo and Bianca acknowledged that they lacked a personal relationship with God and began to live according to His word, they were able to use the help offered by Potter's House to turn their lives around.

As we walked with Ricardo and Bianca, we learned that change comes only from the inside out and only through Jesus, because we were created to have a personal relationship with God through Jesus.

> *On the last and greatest day of the feast, Jesus stood and said in a loud voice, "If anyone is thirsty, let him come to me and drink. Whoever believes in me, as the Scripture has said, streams of living water will flow from within him."*
> **—John 7:37-38 (NASB)**

2. Intellectual Poverty

> *Finally, brothers, whatever is true, whatever is noble, whatever is right, whatever is pure, whatever is lovely, whatever is admirable—if anything is excellent or praiseworthy—think about such things. Whatever you have learned or received or heard from me or seen in me— put it into practice. And the God of peace will be with you.*—**Philippians 4:8-9**

Potter's House defines Intellectual Poverty as *Truth versus Lie*— lack of access to knowledge and living in the shadow of misinformation. The lives of most of our Treasures are steeped in inaccurate assumptions passed down from their parents and grandparents. Because education is a luxury, they continue to live in ignorance. Their culture teaches them that they are worthless like the garbage that surrounds them, and without hope they pass this belief on to their children. One of those children was Claudia Boror, who first came to Potter's House when she was 4-years old.

Claudia's parents were among the first couples who participated in our couples' program. Neither of them had any formal schooling, and they both scavenged in the garbage dump to support Claudia and her five siblings. Their two oldest children had quit school and left home when they were about 16.

Claudia dutifully went to elementary school in the morning and the PHA tutoring program in the afternoon, but the lessons were never easy for her. Her goal was to drop out of school and start working. She, like most of the Treasures, knew no reality other than life in the garbage. She was bogged down in that reality without plans, skills, or a desire for a better life.

By the time Claudia reached junior high, negative thoughts filled her mind.

When the dump is your teacher, the lessons you learn are "I cannot do anything." "I am garbage too." By the time Claudia reached junior high, negative thoughts filled her mind. "Nobody loves me." "I am ugly." "I am unworthy of a better life."

For as he thinks in his heart, so is he.
—Proverbs 23:7a (AMPC)

Now a sullen teenager, she started dressing in all black because that reflected how she felt inside. She had even started drinking alcohol with her friends, because she thought it would help her forget her sadness and misery. Members of the staff of our Education Program spoke with her and with her parents about her behavior and reminded her how much she was loved—not just by her family and teachers, but by the God of the universe.

It didn't happen overnight, but Claudia began to feel loved by God and by all of us. God helped her to change her thinking and behavior. She learned and applied God's truths instead of the lies she learned from her neighbors. She substituted God's truth for the lies of the devil.

Claudia was the first member of her family to graduate from high school, and she will soon receive her degree in business administration. She is married, has a child and works as an administrative assistant for a micro-enterprise organization that gives small-business loans.

Poverty kills dreams and fosters ignorance. It clouds understanding and darkens hearts. Over the years, we have learned that helping people be transformed by the renewing of their minds is the way to combat Intellectual poverty.

> *Do not conform any longer to the pattern of this world but be transformed by the renewing of your mind. Then you will be able to test and approve what God's will is—his good, pleasing and perfect will.*—**Romans 12:2**

3. Poverty of Affection

> *See what great love the Father has lavished on us, that we should be called children of God! And that is what we are!*—**1 John 3:1**

Defined as *Love versus Selfishness*, Poverty of Affection is one of the most pernicious forms of poverty we encountered in the dump community. Love for others was a foreign concept among the people who lived and worked in the garbage in Guatemala City. "Every man (woman, and child) for himself" was the rule by which the Treasures lived.

That selfish attitude is what kept them alive. When you are fighting hundreds of people every day for the best scraps the dump has to offer, you cannot afford to be polite. Your rivals may be your neighbors, but it doesn't matter; love has no place in the dump. Irma Chiquito is a Treasure who learned to love at Potter's House.

> *When you are fighting hundreds of people every day for the best scraps the dump has to offer, you cannot afford to be polite.*

Irma had a hard life. She never went to school and had worked for as long as she could remember—first at home doing chores and from age 9, scavenging in the dump. Abused as a child and in desperate need of love and a better life, Irma left the dump community to start a family when she was 14. Sadly, she traded the abuse of her family for abuse at the hands of her alcoholic husband.

After years of mistreatment, she decided to leave her husband and raise her three daughters alone. So she returned to the garbage dump community and built a small house for her family using scraps of cardboard, wood and metal she found in the dump.

Working in the dump was very difficult. Irma, like her fellow scavengers, had to work in all kinds of weather without access to water or bathrooms.

Still, today, the unstable piles of garbage put the Treasures at risk of being buried alive in the mudslides that occur several times a year, and in their zeal to be first in line when a garbage truck starts to dump its load, scavengers often get run over. The dust, the smells, and the pollution make them sick. And some days there is just not enough garbage to go around, so they fail to make enough to feed their families.

Years of abuse, deprivation and loneliness made Irma a tough, angry woman. She got involved at Potter's House when her children attended our Saturday Kids' Club. She started to volunteer, and it wasn't long before our staff offered her counseling and she joined our discipleship program. God showed her that she was one of His beloved Treasures. She started hearing and believing that God loved her and that through Jesus, she was God's child, adopted into His family. She could call Him "Father." She understood that she was loved.

At Potter's House, the Treasures learn that they are valued by God, no matter what others have told them, and through His love they are able to love and value others appropriately.

When Irma understood God's truth, she began to feel loved, and God started to change her life. She was able to love her daughters as she never could before, and she is no longer bitter and unhappy, because she knows that little-by-little God is healing her.

This is love: not that we loved God, but that he loved us and sent his Son as an atoning sacrifice for our sins.—1 **John 4:10**

Personal or Group Follow-Up

What have you learned from the people you serve that has surprised you? Gladys writes, "our goal was not to remove the Treasures from the garbage but to remove the garbage from their minds." Why might this be a more strategic approach?

᪥

Spiritual Poverty. How can religious people still suffer from Spiritual Poverty?

᪥

Intellectual Poverty. How do inaccurate assumptions passed on by others contribute to our Intellectual Poverty?

᪥

Poverty of Affection. What are some tangible ways in which you can model love for others in an environment where survival has pushed people to look out only for themselves?

CHAPTER 10

Beginning to Understand Poverty (Part Two)

In the previous chapter, we examined the first three forms of poverty—Spiritual Poverty, Intellectual Poverty and Poverty of Affection—all of which have to do with the individual person—body, mind, and spirit. Now let's look at two more that focus on the individual and three that focus on relationships with others.

4. Poverty of the Will

> *Like a city whose walls are broken down is a*
> *man who lacks self-control.*—**Proverbs 25:28**

Poverty of the Will is summed up as *Freedom versus Slavery*. It manifests itself as lack of self-control—the lack of capacity to obey, behave properly, cultivate good habits and be determined to succeed. Many Treasures are enslaved by alcohol and drugs, others by the effects of sexual abuse. They lack the will or the desire to change.

In a place like a garbage dump, where chaos rules, it is difficult for children to learn structure, discipline and self-control. There are no rules for kids who are left home alone while parents work. They roam the streets of the community doing what they please and never learning the discipline they will need if they aspire to a life beyond the garbage. Irene Rosales was one such free-range child.

Irene, who lived in the dump community with her mother and three brothers, was totally lacking in self-control when she joined our Education Program at the age of 11. Her mom worked all day long in the garbage dump, and although Irene and her brothers went to school, there was no one at home to help them with homework—or even require that they do it.

"Coming to Potter's House was a great change in my life," she remembers. "The teachers there required us to be responsible—to study hard and do all of our homework. Through activities and Bible classes, we also learned biblical principles and Christian values."

Irene changed at Potter's House. The angry, undisciplined child who came to us has become a charming, responsible young woman with a servant's heart. She graduated from high school as a certified Kindergarten teacher and now volunteers every November at our community-wide Vacation Bible School.

The angry, undisciplined child who came to us has become a charming, responsible young woman with a servant's heart.

Irene is grateful for the structure and discipline her PHA teachers imposed. "Without Potter's House, my brothers and I would not be the people we are today. We would probably be working in the dump with no hope for the future."

Through the PHA Education Program, children like Irene are learning to make good decisions, to live with structure and to act responsibly. The first generation of young Treasures who came to us is now blessing their own children by teaching them the self-control that will help make them responsible adults.

Christ has set us free: It is for freedom that
Christ has set us free. Stand firm, then, and do
not let yourselves be burdened again by a yoke
of slavery.—**Galatians 5:1**

And He delivered us from the bondage of sin:
Don't you know that when you offer yourselves
to someone to obey him as slaves, you are
slaves to the one whom you obey—whether you
are slaves to sin, which leads to death, or to
obedience, which leads to righteousness? But
thanks be to God that, though you used to be
slaves to sin, you wholeheartedly obeyed the
form of teaching to which you were entrusted.
You have been set free from sin and have become
slaves to righteousness.—**Romans 6:16-18**

Jesus has given us self-control: For God did not give
us a spirit of timidity, but a spirit of power, of love
and of self-discipline.—**2 Timothy 1:7 (NHEB)**

5. Physical Poverty

Dear friend, I pray that you may enjoy good
health and that all may go well with you, even
as your soul is getting along well.—**3 John 1:2**

When we identified Physical Poverty, we defined it as *Health versus Sickness.* The Treasures suffer from malnutrition and poor health; they don't get to enjoy the proper functioning of the marvelous body God has given them.

Every day scavengers are exposed to a high-risk environment that causes severe respiratory, gastrointestinal and skin diseases. In addition to the air pollution caused by a steady stream of garbage trucks, methane gas created by decomposing garbage bubbles up to the surface of the dump, further poisoning the air. As they paw through the garbage, the Treasures suffer cuts and scrapes that quickly become infected. And because their water is not purified nor their homes sanitary, they suffer almost constantly from gastrointestinal ailments.

As they paw through the garbage, the Treasures suffer cuts and scrapes that quickly become infected.

Harsh working and living conditions combine to ensure that the Treasures seldom enjoy good health, and without the resources needed to pay for care when illness strikes, most of them neglect their physical health—often until it is too late. Olga Martinez is one example of a Treasure suffering from Physical Poverty.

Olga had a tortilla-making business and was delivering tortillas house-to-house when she fell and injured her knee. The injury was not very serious, but while treating it, a doctor discovered that she also had a tumor in that leg, and ultimately, she had to have her leg amputated.

Years later, she went to the medical clinic at Potter's House because she had a respiratory infection, and while she was there the conversation turned to the way she walked and the revelation of the need for a new prosthesis. Her old prosthesis was on the verge of falling apart, and because she had lost weight, it did not fit anymore; it was so loose that she had to stuff it with rags so it would not fall off.

It had gotten so bad that Olga gave up wearing the prosthesis at home and decided to wear it only to attend church and her discipleship group at PHA. She prayed that the prosthesis would not break while she was away from home and leave her stranded.

A physician volunteering at Potter's House met Olga and learned of her plight. God moved his heart, and he offered to buy her a new prosthesis. She was overwhelmed by his kindness. All she had asked God was that her prosthesis would last a little longer. She never dreamed of asking Him for a new prosthesis, because she thought she was unworthy of such a wonderful gift.

During the whole process of getting the new prosthesis, she felt loved by the staff and the American physician. The new prosthesis he chose was one of the best. Very lightweight and made of titanium, it had a skin-colored cosmetic cover that made Olga feel good about her appearance. In expressing her thanks to the doctor, she said, "Your generosity has filled my heart with joy and gratitude to the Lord."

At Potter's House we teach the Treasures when to seek medical care and how to eat well. We have a full-time doctor on staff plus a pharmacy and many volunteer medical personnel. Our Nutrition Program provides a nutritious lunch for our kids every school day, teaching them that good food can taste just as good as junk food. We remind them that their bodies are sacred and valuable.

> *Do you not know that your bodies are temples of the Holy Spirit, who is in you, whom you have received from God? You are not your own; you were bought at a price. Therefore honor God with your bodies.*—**1 Corinthians 6:19-20**

6. Poverty of Support Network

*Two are better than one because they have a
good return for their work: If one falls down,
his friend can help him up. But pity the man
who falls and has no one to help him up!*

—Ecclesiastes 4:9-12

Poverty of Support Network is defined as *Family versus Loneliness*.
Many Treasures lack close family or community support. They
feel alone—not just within their often-dysfunctional families
but in the broader community as well. They feel that they have
no one with whom to share the joys and challenges of daily
living, no place where they belong. Before he died at the age of
96, Don Desiderio Carias told us his story.

My name is Desiderio Carias. I live alone in a
small shack in one of the neighborhoods
around the garbage dump. I was married for 35
years, but my wife and I never had children,
and now that my wife
is gone, I have no one. I
am alone. Living alone is
not easy, especially at my
age, because I am too sick
and weak to work.

*At night when I am
in pain, I worry
that I may die, and
no one will notice.*

I used to be a mason, but
now I have no income. At night when I am in pain,
I worry that I may die, and no one will notice. I
often feel lonely and sad.

I am very grateful that I am now part of Potter's
House. They are my new family. They helped

me put a new roof on my little house so I can stay dry during the rainy season. They love me and give a helping hand by providing medicine when I am sick, companionship when I am lonely, words of encouragement when I am discouraged, and food to keep me alive.

The Treasures—especially the elderly—often feel abandoned and neglected. Potter's House is a place where they can get a nutritious meal and enjoy the company of people who love them. PHA volunteers built Don Desiderio a warm, dry house, and the staff found a family that was happy to share the house and care for him.

At Potter's House, our holistic approach offers God's Treasures, the support they need, so they never have to feel alone. We are practicing God's love and remembering the words of Jesus in Acts 20:35: "It is more blessed to give than to receive."

God sets the lonely in families.—**Psalm 68:6a**

7. Poverty of Civic Involvement

> *Also, seek the peace and prosperity of the city to which I have carried you into exile. Pray to the LORD for it, because if it prospers, you too will prosper.*—**Jeremiah 29:7**

Poverty of Civic Involvement—*Participation versus Indifference*—is one of the less-obvious forms of poverty. Although they live very close to their neighbors, many Treasures have no interest in getting involved in what we might call community affairs—efforts to make life better for everyone.

Leadership, cooperation and collaboration within a community are simply not part of their culture. The result is that the every-man-for-himself mentality ensures that positive change comes slowly, and life, in general, remains chaotic. Aury Guzman assumed leadership in her community when none of her neighbors was willing to step up.

When she came to live in the garbage dump area in 1988, all of Aury's neighbors lived in small shacks without potable water, electricity, sewers or paved streets. Squabbles among neighbors were very common and made life even harder.

In 1998, the Guatemala City government started to organize a committee to represent in the dump community and bring some order to the area. The municipal leaders invited a representative of that committee to attend meetings where such important matters as access to potable water and installation of sewers were discussed. Aury has been a respected member of this committee for approximately 22 years.

> Because my neighbors were unwilling to participate, I agreed to serve and was named president of the committee. I accepted the responsibility even though I knew nothing about being a leader. I have only a 6th grade education, and I was terrified of speaking in public.

> Potter's House supported the community leaders, and in 2004, they invited me to participate in training. They began by teaching us very basic things: how to prepare an agenda for a productive meeting, how to speak in public, how to write letters to request support and how to write progress reports. I learned a lot!

Working on projects with teams of American volunteers was a great challenge for me, but Potter's House helped me grow. I could not believe how my neighbors got involved and worked together when they saw me leading in the way.

Working on projects with teams of American volunteers was a great challenge for me, but Potter's House helped me grow

Potter's House has taught us to care more about one another. For example, when a family is chosen to receive a house or other blessing, Potter's House helps me deal with the envy of their neighbors and supports me when I encourage those neighbors to work alongside the family and the volunteers to build the house.

Potter's House relies on the community leaders when interfacing with the community, always emphasizing the importance of loving one another and inspiring neighbors to care about the welfare of others. And it's working. By God's grace the infrastructure of many of the neighborhoods has improved dramatically, hundreds of new homes have been built, and countless squabbles, large and small, have been resolved.

What the leaders have learned has affected their families and their neighborhoods; they can now value others just as God values all of us.

A new command I give you: Love one another.
As I have loved you, so you must love one another.
—John 13:34

8. Economic Poverty

*If there is a poor man with you, one of your
brothers, in any of your towns in your land
which the LORD your God is giving you, you
shall not harden your heart, nor close your hand
from your poor brother; but you shall freely open
your hand to him, and shall generously lend him
sufficient for his need in whatever he lacks.*
—Deuteronomy 15:7-8 (NASB)

Economic Poverty, what most people think of when hear the
word "poverty" is the most obvious form of poverty. Just about
anyone can tell when a person or family is surrounded by
Scarcity versus Abundance.

On a good day, the Treasures who scavenge in the dump
earn about $5, but their average daily income is about $2. At that
rate, progress and growth are impossible, and our Treasures
never have more than they need to get through the day. Aura
Marina Muñoz is a Treasure who has worked hard to escape
from Economic Poverty.

I am 50-years old, and I live with my four children. Since I was little, I dreamed of being a
hair stylist, but I left school after 1ˢᵗ grade and
started working cleaning
houses when I was just
10-years old.

*Some days I had to
tell my children to go
to bed early, because
I did not have
anything to feed
them for dinner.*

My husband left me when
our fourth child was born,
and I worked very hard to
support my kids, but I didn't
make enough money to

provide three meals a day for them. Some days I had to tell my children to go to bed early, because I did not have anything to feed them for dinner. They often cried themselves to sleep.

A friend invited me to Potter's House, and I was able to enroll my children in the Education Program, which helped them do better in school and provided a nutritious lunch every school day. I learned that I could call on PHA in times of distress.

Because of an accident I suffered more than ten years ago, I have a serious degenerative condition in my knee, which makes it very painful to walk long distances and do physical work. I was afraid I would not be able to work to support my children.

Then, in 2009, PHA gave me the opportunity to participate in a beauty course, learning to cut and style hair. I graduated from their program and started to work as a hairstylist in my home. Not only has my dream come true, but I now have a way to continue providing for my family. I thank God for all the people at Potter's House, because through them God has given me strength and opportunities to give my children hope for a better life.

Two of Aura Marina's children have graduated from high school, and the other two are doing well in school. She is a leader of a project that pays women to make Teddy bears that are sold in the U.S.

Her cheerful demeanor and her willingness to work hard make her an inspiration for other Treasures, and she has learned to share with those who are in need, because there is no one so poor that they cannot share with others.

Over the years, we have learned that working to overcome poverty is a very complex task. But rather than simply addressing Economic Poverty, Potter's House is empowering the Treasures and equipping them to overcome all eight forms of poverty.

And now, brothers, we want you to know about the grace that God has given the Macedonian churches. Out of the most severe trial, their overflowing joy and their extreme poverty welled up in rich generosity. For I testify that they gave as much as they were able, and even beyond their ability. Entirely on their own.

—2 Corinthians 8:1-3

Personal or Group Follow-Up

Poverty of the Will. Why might rules and schedules be helpful for people who suffer from Poverty of the Will?

⌁

Physical Poverty. Why might "Health" be a better way to describe Physical Poverty than "Sickness"?

⌁

Poverty of Support Network. What support networks exist in your life that are also important for people living in poverty to have?

⌁

Poverty of Civic Involvement. What positive changes take place in a person's life when they begin to participate in bringing about change for their community?

⌁

Economic Poverty. What is the danger of defining poverty only in terms of economic scarcity?

⌁

Which of the Eight Forms of Poverty do you find most difficult to address in your community? Why?

⌁

Which of the personal stories in this chapter impacted you the most? Why?

CHAPTER 11

A Blessing in Disguise

"Potter's House is on fire!" Awakened from a deep sleep at 3:00 a.m., my husband, Edgar, heard those horrifying words. It was May 6, 1997, and the person guarding our facilities had called to say, "I have bad news to share with you. Potter's House is on fire, so please come as soon as possible."

Still in shock, we jumped into our clothes and headed to the dump. When we arrived, we couldn't park our car anywhere near our property because it was surrounded by people and fire trucks—eight of them. Firefighters were hard at work battling the flames that had engulfed our wooden structure.

As we walked toward the property, we discovered that people who knew us and Potter's House were guarding the area to ensure that others would not take advantage of the situation and rob us. It touched our hearts to see them opening up a path through the crowd and telling us, "Don't worry. We are taking care of PHA's belongings."

Although it was very dark, we could see that the entire carpentry shop had burned, and the rooms where we stored food and teaching materials were completely destroyed.

Our Work Was in Ashes

Surrounded by neighbors who stored recycled materials and flammable substances in their little shacks, the risk of fire was always present, but it was a risk that we at PHA were willing to take. That night, the fear became a reality, and in just 30 minutes, the work of the past ten years was reduced to ashes.

Edgar remembers, "At such times, we tend to think the worst. During those moments of chaos, we were afraid that besides losing our building to the fire, we had to worry about people trying to steal our few remaining possessions. But the Lord was faithful, and amid that chaos, we saw that the Treasures were not trying to steal from us. Instead, they were helping us by fighting the fire and by forming a human chain to salvage our belongings."

I wrapped myself in a blanket and sat down to watch until the sun came up.

I could not move. I wrapped myself in a blanket and sat down to watch until the sun came up. I remembered how God had provided everything and wondered why He had allowed it to be destroyed.

The ministry had faced many challenges, including limited resources, understaffing, and the overwhelming needs of the Treasures. We had been asking God for a "Time of resting." Instead, I felt like we were moving from one trial to a worse one.

I felt as if I had lost a friend or family member. But even as I began to grieve, God began to clear my thoughts, and I came to understand that He had not willed the property to burn. Our facilities were made of wood and small plastic houses that an organization had donated. I realized that the fire had a purpose, and instead of focusing on what we had lost, I began to focus on what we hadn't lost.

I was able to see the love of God shining through all the people of the dump community. They helped us to clean up. Later a neighbor donated blocks, and others came to pray for us and offered to help us begin construction.

Sometimes, an incident like this can be interpreted as a sign of the end of a ministry. But God did not allow it. Looking back, I can see that it was the beginning of a new era—an era of safer, more permanent facilities.

> *An incident like this can be interpreted as a sign of the end of a ministry.*

I saw God working in many ways. An unexplainable event brought an unexplainable way to build new and better facilities. He tested the faith of many of us as leaders of the ministry and staff, but now, we can say that the fire was a blessing in disguise. We remained obedient and stayed committed to serving the Treasures. The Lord answered our prayers and sent people to support the construction of the new facilities—all made of concrete block.

Five Phases of Rebuilding

The process was divided into five phases. The first phase was to build the wall around the property and give the structure a face on the street. We created a facade with three entrances, one for people, one for cars, and one for buses and trucks. The goal was to provide a secure place to keep our supplies and equipment.

The second phase was the addition of 10 bathrooms. Prior to this, we had only one restroom, and building more was an urgent need. Upon completion of this stage, the staff members immediately felt more comfortable.

During the third phase, we built a four-story administration building, which would house offices for program coordinators and fund-raising staff, meeting rooms, and the volunteer's room—a huge improvement over the former rooms of wood and tin. The fourth phase saw the addition of a huge multipurpose room and a commercial kitchen.

Previously, our maximum capacity was 100 people at a time; in the new space, we were able to host up to 500 for activities that included daily lunches, emergency shelter, weddings, evangelistic activities, parties for children, sports clinics, Vacation Bible Schools, graduations, medical clinics, and many other events that have benefited the community.

Phase five was a temporary wooden annex of 12 classrooms that provided learning space for 300 children who were part of our daily tutoring program.

The process took seven years to complete. The Lord was faithful in sending many friends and supporters who donated the resources so that even during this challenging time of rapid growth, PHA never had to take out a mortgage. In 2004 we moved into the new facilities.

Finally, in 2017 the Lord allowed us to replace the "temporary" wooden education annex with a beautiful permanent addition where children can learn and focus on futures beyond the garbage.

The fire was truly a blessing in disguise. The construction of a permanent facility on the edge of the garbage dump has improved the capacity, quality and impact of our work. We are using the facilities to build hope for tomorrow.

> *We know that in everything God works for*
> *the good of those who love him. They are the*
> *people he called, because that was his plan.*
>
> **—Romans 8:28 (NCV)**

Personal or Group Follow-Up

How have you seen God work through the "ashes" in your own life or ministry?

⤸

What does it mean for you to focus on what you have, rather than on what you may have lost?

⤸

What unexplainable events has God used to bring about unexplainable blessings in your life?

Additional Resources

Unexplainable: Pursuing a Life Only God Can Make Possible. Don Cousins. David C. Cook. 2009.

CHAPTER 12

Serving and Learning from the Treasures

Walking among the Treasures and the squalid shacks in which they lived, I was overwhelmed by the poverty and hardship surrounding me. Their homes were made of scraps—corrugated metal, cardboard, wood, and plastic—that they had scavenged from the dump. Likewise, the furnishings were castoffs found in other people's garbage. Most families slept together on a single filthy mattress on the floor.

The floors were dirt that turned to mud during the rainy season, and without secure doors and windows, rats and other vermin shared their living space. The fortunate had access to a communal shower—a tiny space tucked between houses with a hose for washing and a curtain for a door. The filth of the non-flushing communal toilets was unspeakable.

Like many of the volunteers and workers who came after me, I fell into a trap; I had a Messiah complex. I believed that I had to solve the Treasures' problems in order to alleviate their suffering. Over and over, I asked myself, "How can I help them?" "How can I provide for their needs?" "How can I do anything?" Although I had more resources than the Treasures, I certainly did not have enough to lift them from poverty by myself. I felt impotent and useless.

I was even disappointed with God, because He had called me to serve the poor, to be His hands and feet, but I believed

He had failed by not equipping me to do the job. It never occurred to me that He had equipped me perfectly to do exactly what He wanted me to do.

As I got to know my new friends and gained a better understanding of their situation, I began to learn from them. It was very humbling to be reminded that I was not God and could not, therefore, solve the Treasures' problems. The Treasures in the dump community taught me many lessons about faith and trust in God. When they were sick, they did not run to a doctor or a pharmacy to get medicine, they prayed for healing. Because their resources were so limited, they had no choice but to trust God every day for food and shelter for their families.

Because their resources were so limited, they had no choice but to trust God every day for food and shelter for their families.

If they had a good day scavenging in the dump, they could buy a little extra for the evening meal. If they had a bad day and came home empty-handed, they made do with what they had and prayed for a better day tomorrow.

Every family's needs were different, and each of them had a story of suffering—a son born disabled, a daughter killed in an accident, a father shot by gang members, an elderly parent dead of a treatable disease, a young mother abandoned with a house full of kids. Their suffering and their need were so great that I begged God to use me to make their lives better.

We quickly learned, that we had to focus our limited time and resources, so Lisbeth and I decided that the best way to effect change in the community was to minister to the children—the next generation that could lead their families and their community out of poverty. Most of the adults were set in their ways; many had lost hope. The children, however, were still able to dream of a better tomorrow.

A Life Transformed

One of the first children we invested in was Aury Sandoval, who was just 8-years old when she got her first job, collecting garbage from the homes of slightly wealthier people. Her payment was food, usually just stale bread, but it was often more than she got at home. She was the daughter of an alcoholic father and a hard-working mother who did her best to support Aury and her four brothers.

Aury was 10-years old the first time her father took her to the dump. Her job was to help her mom take care of the family's "stall," the place where her dad brought the things he found during the day for safe-keeping. Although she herself was not scavenging, it was still a dirty and dangerous place for a child.

Aury's mother, Juliana, understood the value of education and did everything she could to enable her children to go to school so they could have a better future. Guatemalan school children attend classes for only half a day, but even a few hours away from the dump can diminish the family's income for that day.

Having no money to buy school supplies, Juliana made a notebook for Aury out of relatively clean paper she found in the dump. She stitched the pages together by hand and made a serviceable notebook for her daughter. Eager to learn and find out what education was all

Having no money to buy school supplies, Juliana made a notebook for Aury out of relatively clean paper she found in the dump.

about, Aury set off for her first day of school. But her young spirit was quickly crushed.

On the playground, her classmates refused to play with her. They knew where she lived and told her they didn't want to play with garbage like her. In the classroom, they pulled out their store-bought supplies and made fun of the new girl's makeshift notebook. Aury was embarrassed and ashamed.

Despite the feelings of inferiority and rejection that she experienced in school, Aury never gave up. Neither did Juliana, who supported her daughter through elementary school and proudly attended her graduation from 6th grade.

But Aury's path was not smooth. Conditions in her home had not changed, and she carried a great deal of bitterness in her heart. Because her future had really not changed, death was constantly on her mind; when she was alone, she even played that she was dying.

A Life-Changing Invitation

Then, in 1992, a group of volunteers from Potter's House visited the community, inviting young people to attend our Youth Program. Fearing more rejection, Aury said she wasn't interested. But the Lord had heard her cries and was working through those patient, loving volunteers. Sensing the pain in her heart, they spent time with her and eventually succeeded in getting her to accept their invitation.

Aury remembers, "I will never forget that special day!" That Saturday they were celebrating a Quinceañera, an elaborate 15th birthday party that all Guatemalan girls dream about. "To be honest, I stayed because of the food. I was hungry, and never in my life had I seen such a big cake that you could actually eat.

For the first time in 13 years, I felt loved, accepted and respected—by both adults and other kids. That party, which touched my heart deeply, was the beginning of God's transformation in my life. You have no idea how good I felt that afternoon! It was incredible to feel sincere hugs from people I didn't know—people who didn't care about my dirty clothes or the smell of garbage that was stamped on my body."

When Aury started high school, Juliana told her that she could no longer help her financially with her studies. Aury replied confidently that she would pay for her own schooling. So, she went job hunting. The only job she could find was in a recycling workshop, removing labels and washing bottles. From sunrise to sunset—many days from 2:00 or 3:00 a.m. until 6:00 p.m.—she stood at her station cleaning the bottles that had been found in the dump by scavengers.

She worked hard for years, determined to realize her dream of a life beyond the garbage. She went to school from 7:00 to 9:00 p.m. with no vacation or days off. Her schedule left little time for homework, so many mornings she left for work with bitter tears in her eyes, having failed to complete her assignments.

The Easy Way Out

On the weekends, she made time to go to Potter's House, where she learned about the love of God. But she struggled to understand how the Lord, if He truly loved her, could allow her to live "such a miserable life." Life was so hard for Aury that she eventually decided to take what seemed to be the easy way out. The people in her

The people in her community who seemed to have the most money and receive the most respect were the gang members.

community who seemed to have the most money and receive the most respect were the gang members. So she decided to join the infamous MS-13 gang.

On the eve of her initiation, which involved being raped by the members of the gang, she found herself sitting in the back row of one of the small churches that dot the dump community. In tears, she cried out to the God she had heard about at Potter's House, "If you are real, save me from this initiation and this life." As she prayed, she was overwhelmed with a feeling of warmth and well-being. She knew God was real and that she did not have to join the gang, even though backing out of an initiation was very dangerous.

Aury recommitted herself to her studies and her time at Potter's House. "The Lord, through PHA, gave me the opportunity to change my way of thinking." He gave her several "gifts"—extraordinary opportunities to change her life. First, she found a better job. Then, after graduating from high school, she received a scholarship to one of our universities here in Guatemala.

She was working at Potter's House and going to college part time when she was invited to spend six weeks in the United States to have a transcultural experience and learn English. She made many friends and learned a lot about American culture, but she never became accustomed to the strange American desire to take warm showers. Neither could she fathom their penchant for putting clothes on their small dogs.

When she returned to Guatemala, she married a fellow PHA employee, named Eddy, gave birth to a baby boy, and while maintaining a job and a home, earned a master's degree in human resources. Now she has two sons, and she and Eddy have their own ministry serving at-risk youth.

Reflecting on her youth, Aury says, "the best gift Potter's House gave me was getting to know Jesus as my Savior. It has changed my future, here on earth and also in heaven. "Now I am a different person—spiritually, intellectually and financially. Potter's House gave me the opportunity to dream again after the reality of life in the dump community had drained me of hope. Now I expect the best each day in all the areas of my life. I give thanks to the Lord for being so good to me! And to Potter's House, thank you for discovering a Treasure in me!"

What a joy it was for me to attend Aury's wedding and to be there when she received her master's degree! It had taken many years, but in Aury and a handful of other Treasures, I saw the fulfillment of God's promise to me. He had, indeed, equipped me and the PHA staff to change lives and lift His precious Treasures from the garbage.

> *Listen, my dear brothers: has not God chosen those who are poor in the eyes of the world to be rich in faith and to inherit the kingdom he promised those who love him?*—**James 2:5**

Personal or Group Follow-Up

How do you resolve the tension of genuinely wanting to help others without falling into the trap of trying to fix all of their problems?

⮎

In what ways are you tempted to rely more upon your own knowledge, skills and capacity than upon God?

⮎

If you know Jesus, how has He changed your life here on earth and in heaven?

Additional Resources

Seeing What Is Sacred: Becoming More Spiritually Sensitive to the Everyday Moments of Life. Ken Gire. Thomas Nelson, Inc. 2006

CHAPTER 13

In the Potter's Hands

"I would like to buy a pound of clay."

"I'm sorry, we don't sell clay."

"Aren't you a pottery store?"

"No, we are not."

"So, why do you have the name Potter's House?"

Our receptionist grew weary of the conversation, but eventually people caught on.

Why did we choose the name Potter's House? In January of 1993, when we registered as a nonprofit organization in Guatemala, the first act of our first board of directors was to choose a name. The Lord put in the heart of Jodi Hammer, one of the members, the idea of calling the ministry "Potter's House," based on Jeremiah 18:1-6.

Reading and studying those Bible verses helped us to understand the role of a potter. God also revealed to us through interaction with those verses one of the core values of our ministry. We wanted to acknowledge that He was the potter—the One with the vision and the skill to make something out of nothing.

In addition to Jeremiah, Isaiah and Zechariah present the picture of the potter and the clay in the Old Testament. In the New Testament, we have Paul in Romans 9:21 reminding us that God is the potter and we are the clay.

Early in our history, we took the staff to the home of a potter in Totonicapán (six hours from Guatemala City). Things were much more rustic and primitive there, so we were able to get close and watch the potter make a vessel of clay. As in the Bible, the finished product required the potter, the clay, and the wheel.

In modern times, the wheel is turned by an electric motor, but the speed of the wheel is still controlled by the foot of the potter while his hands shape what will become a work of art. God the Potter is the same, using His capable hands, guided by His supreme intelligence, to mold and shape the clay into the vessel that will serve Him best.

Among the lessons we have learned from studying the passage in Jeremiah are the following.

God invites us to join His ministry

This is the word that came to Jeremiah from the Lord.—**vs.1**

In this first verse, it is clear that God looked for Jeremiah; Jeremiah was not looking for God. No one who has come to serve at Potter's House has come by chance. God, the Potter, has brought all of us here, even those who don't yet know Him.

He has chosen each of us with a specific purpose in mind, and he has stirred the heart of each one who has come. In John 15:16 Jesus says, "you did not choose me, but I chose you and appointed you so that you might go and bear fruit—fruit that will last—and so that whatever you ask in my name the Father will give you." You will bear fruit that will last!

God will speak to you at Potter's House

Go down to the potter's house, and there I will
give you my message.—**vs.2**

Go down! It is a call to action. *Go down!* It is a call to service. Potter's House is not a social club or place to hang out with friends. It is a center of action and service to God, and it is a place where He will speak to you.

Stay alert! God will speak to you through many channels and by many means. Don't worry about the channel or the means; the important thing to know is that God has a special message for you at Potter's House. It was clear when He told Jeremiah that He would make His voice heard through the potter. The same Potter will to speak to you.

> *The important thing to know is that God has a special message for you at Potter's House.*

Potter's House is a place of transformation

So I went down to the potter's house and I saw
Him working at the wheel.—**vs. 3**

Went down. In addition to the obvious geographical meaning of that phrase, we can also interpret it as a command to humble yourself. Jeremiah was obedient, went down and humbled himself. Potter's House may not be the place to which you expected God would send you, but by serving there, you are being obedient.

The potter was working at the wheel. He was working on the pot. The potter controls the wheel, using it to shape the vessel. God uses trials and circumstances to mold and shape us.

God is working. Your life will be transformed as you serve Him. He is transforming not only the lives of the Treasures but also the lives of the staff, volunteers and supporters who serve them on His behalf.

Most of the time, when seeking guidance, we do not look down, we look up. We look up to someone—someone successful, with more experience—to advise us. We look for the best of the best. How surprised would you be to learn that your adviser was a scavenger who works in a garbage dump? In Proverbs 6:6, we learn that guidance can come even from an insect: "Go to the ant, you sluggard. Consider its ways and be wise."

Please do not misunderstand me. I am not saying that you should not try to find the best help you can. I am advising you to open your heart and mind so you can hear God's voice and be willing to learn from others. I met God in a very unexpected place, and you can too.

Potter's House is a place where God will shape you

But the pot he was shaping from the clay
was marred in his hands; so the potter formed
it into another pot, shaping it as seemed best
to him.—**vs. 4**

He is the Potter, we are the clay, and we are in his hands. God the Potter has absolute power over the clay. He can make any type of vessel He pleases. The destiny of the clay—its beauty, its utility, its value—is in His hands from the very beginning.

God the Potter has absolute power over the clay. He can make any type of vessel He pleases.

To prepare the clay for the wheel, the potter works it with his hands, breaking down any hard lumps and eliminating bubbles that would compromise the integrity of the vessel. He patiently kneads it, seeking just the right texture and color, all the while making it an expression of his love. Although his goal is beautiful, the process can be painful for the clay.

Suffering is a normal part of life, and most people flee from it. We have to change that concept. At Potter's House, we see much suffering among the Treasures, their families, and their communities. Unfortunately, there is little most of them can do to alleviate their own physical woes, and apart from a relationship with Jesus it is difficult for them to find any joy in their lives.

I was not immune to that feeling of hopelessness. Faced with the reality of unrelieved suffering in the lives of my friends, many times I wondered whether even God could change people afflicted with such poverty. I didn't know how to process the pain I felt when I heard the Treasures' stories. As I struggled with their overwhelming need, I learned that I was not the Messiah; I was not God.

Right about the time I was writing this chapter God taught me about *the lament.* Lament is used in the Bible, particularly in many of the Psalms, but even more famously in the book of Lamentations. Mark Vroegop, pastor of College Park Church in Indianapolis comments that "lament is the honest cry of an aching heart struggling with the paradox of suffering in light of the promise of God's goodness."

Lament is not just crying out in the face of evil, nor is it ignoring pain because we know that God is good. Instead, it is responding honestly to the paradox of God's goodness and our pain. In this sense, Vroegop adds, "Crying is human; lamenting is Christian."

Lament is the language of suffering. Most of us do not know how to respond to our own pain, much less that of others. Lament does not seek to resolve the problem, nor does it necessarily seek to encourage the person in pain to recover their smile. Instead, it seeks to describe and verbalize the internal pain in a manner consistent with the teachings of the Bible.

While I am writing this book, Covid-19 is affecting my country and the world. Reading those Psalms of lament has helped me to express my pain to the Lord. Consider the words of Psalm 6:6-7:

> *I am worn out from my groaning.*
> *All night long I flood my bed with weeping*
> *and drench my couch with tears.*
> *My eyes grow weak with sorrow.*
> *they fail because of all my foes.*

I have felt what David describes here, but I never knew how pray to God the way he does. Lament gives us the words we need. Without lamenting amid suffering, our prayers risk insincerity and superficiality as we attempt to express joy in a painful situation.

Lament helps us identify with those who suffer. When we lament with someone, we do not trivialize their pain by talking about the goodness of God. Rather, we empathize with them sincerely and, with that understanding, explain the hope of the gospel.

As we have served the Treasures, all of the Potter's House staff have experienced pain. Many of us have had to deal simultaneously with pain in our own lives. Reading the words of lament in the Bible gives us a language that points us to God's goodness and mercy and gives us

> *As we have served the Treasures, all of the Potter's House staff have experienced pain.*

hope that He is working in ways that we do not expect—ways that will use the pain for good, transforming our lives and making us more like Jesus.

God humbles us and tests us so we can learn what is really in our hearts as we go through those trials and sufferings.

> *Remember how the Lord your God led you all the way in the wilderness these forty years, to humble and test you in order to know what was in your heart, whether or not you would keep his commands.*—**Deuteronomy 8:2**

Be encouraged, make an effort, even if it seems that your life has been spoiled. We are in the hands of the Potter. God cares for us. After suffering, we will be different; we will be better.

As Paul tells us in Romans 9:21, "The thing molded will not say to the molder, 'Why did you make me like this,' will it?" (NASB)

Potter's House is a place where you are in His hand

Then the word of the Lord came to me: He said, "can't I do the same thing with you?" Says the Lord. "You are in my hands like the clay in the potter's hands."—**vs. 5-6**

You can see the Potter's patience and love while with the clay is in his hands.

God desires to lift us to the highest level he made us to attain. If you refuse to let Him do that, He will make another vessel. He will make you as good as you allow Him to. By the Potter's touch, we are transformed into beautiful and valuable vessels. We bear the imprint of the Master's hand. As we view ourselves through His eyes and feel His touch, we learn what sort of vessel He wants us to become.

Clearly, Potter's House is not the only place where God can shape you, but you must be brave enough to put yourself in His hands—in a situation in which transformation can occur. Be alert and ask yourself: What is my Potter's House? Where is God leading me? What is keeping me from going there?

Potter's House is God's idea

God has a vision, a very clear idea of what He wants for His people who live in poverty. Potter's House is only one of the tools he uses to realize his goals for them. Other people and organizations may approach the realization of His goals in different ways, but the goals are always His.

> *God has a vision, a very clear idea of what He wants for His people who live in poverty.*

"Your Kingdom come; your will be done." God wants to do His will in and through all people. Are we loyal subjects of His Kingdom? The most important role of Potter's House is to establish the Kingdom of God among the poor in Guatemala.

The Lord in His love is molding us. He wants us to live an abundant life for His purposes and glory. God exposes us to unexpected events in unexpected ways where we can meet Him.

> *But now, O Lord, You are our Father. We are the clay, and You our potter; And all of us are the work of Your hand.*—**Isaiah 64:8 (NASB)**

Embrace what God is calling you to, because He is the Potter and we are the clay. If you do that and join us at Potter's House, you will say, as so many of us have over the years: After serving at the Potter's House you will never be the same.

> *Can't I do the same thing with you? Says the Lord. You are in my hands like the clay in the potter's hands.*—**Jeremiah 18:6 (NCV)**

Personal or Group Follow-Up

What is the meaning behind your organization's name? Are you living it out in how you act and what you do?

⟿

How does a better understanding of *lament* help you better accompany people in pain and suffering?

⟿

Where and how is God is shaping you? Are you brave enough to put yourself in His hands and allow Him to transform you?

Additional Resources

For more thoughts on lamenting see Mark Vroegop's sermon series on the book of Lamentations: yourchurch.com/series/lamentations-dark-clouds-deep-mercy

Dark Clouds, Deep Mercy: Discovering the Grace of Lament. Mark Vroegop. Crossway. 2019.

A Sacred Sorrow: Reaching Out to God in the Lost Language of Lament. Michael Card. NavPress. 2005.

CHAPTER 14

Love and Passion Are Not Enough

It was our wedding day, and the news was bad.

My groom, Edgar Güitz, was named director of Potter's House in July of 1996 and immediately set about evaluating the previous five years of ministry. Several hours before our wedding on August 24, he presented a report on that evaluation to our board of directors. His report concluded that given the trend of our finances, the ministry would have to close by the end of the year.

Like a good husband, he kept the sad news from me until after the honeymoon.

The ministry was in bad financial shape, but I didn't have a clue. I didn't know how to read financial statements, and my management skills were lacking. Although I received periodic reports from our accountant, I didn't know how to interpret them.

Edgar's analysis revealed the source of the problem. The church that had been supplying 80% of our budget had split, and the result of that split was a significant decrease in their support of Potter's House.

Lisbeth had been on sabbatical that year. After ten years of hard pioneer work, the board had approved desperately needed sabbaticals for Lisbeth and me. Since we couldn't both go at the same time, Lisbeth took her sabbatical first. At the end of that year, Lisbeth concluded that she needed a change in her life, and she resigned.

My plan was to use my sabbatical year to enjoy life as a newlywed. But Edgar asked me to postpone my sabbatical year and continue working at Potter's House. Of course, I wanted to help my husband, the new director, so I put my long-awaited sabbatical on hold.

He also asked me to change roles. For ten years, I had been serving the community directly—teaching the children, praying with families and offering other help as needed. Now, Edgar asked me to launch a new area in the ministry and do fundraising. I was the only English speaker on the team at that time, so I was the only one who could communicate with our donors in the U.S.

My first thought was that fund-raising equals money, and money is not a ministry. Ministry happens when one serves others directly. I did not believe that fund-raising could be a ministry.

> *I did not believe that fund-raising could be a ministry.*

It was going to be a big challenge for me. In His mercy, the Lord opened a door for me to take some training in fund-raising during which I learned and understood that fund-raising was, in fact, an important ministry. Everything that we do in the name of Jesus and for Him is a ministry, whether it is preaching, medical care, teaching, accounting, building maintenance... or fund-raising.

I learned that in the Christian worldview, fund-raising should be viewed as inviting people to join what God is doing in His ministry. This new role gave me an opportunity to tell people what God was doing among the Treasures and to invite them into relationship with Potter's House. For more than 20 years, the relationships I have built with our supporters have been an "exchange of blessings." They have blessed me, and I believe I have blessed them. What a privilege it has been for me to pray for them!

The lesson I learned in my new position is that love and passion are not enough to accomplish God's work. To do His work and accomplish His will, it is essential to understand what God is calling us to do, even if that task does not seem like ministry to us. If we accept the challenge to use the gifts He has given us, we can help take our ministry to the next level—the level that God wants for His glory and the expansion of His kingdom.

God's Stewards

Facing desperate needs, especially in my country, which has a lot of poverty and not a lot of government help—for either the poor or the nonprofits that serve them—was overwhelming. As directors, we didn't know where to go to find the information and training we needed to equip us to run a Christian nonprofit organization successfully. All the information available in my country dealt with running a business—making money. No one was interested in learning how to help people who could not pay for their services.

Imagine, then, our excitement when a foundation invited us to the United States for training and offered to pay all our expenses. At first, we declined the invitation, thinking that we would rather use the money they were offering to improve programs that would benefit the Treasures.

But, no; that wasn't the deal. The people at the foundation explained that they were confident that what they were offering was much more valuable than money. They wanted to train us to be the best possible stewards of the Lord's ministry. So, we accepted the invitation.

We soon realized that both Edgar and I desperately needed that training, and in 2000, while we were there, we learned about the Christian Leadership Alliance (CLA), an organization that has been equipping Christian leaders for Kingdom impact for more than 44 years.

In retrospect, the Lord was answering our anxious prayers with His provision, which was, to our surprise, not money. He was giving us the tools we needed to run a successful Christian nonprofit ministry for His glory.

> *The Lord was answering our anxious prayers with His provision,*

CLA offers an accreditation, and in 2011 I became a Credentialed Christian Nonprofit Leader (CCNL), participating regularly in their ongoing program of learning and growing. They train nonprofit leaders in areas like governance, communication, fund-raising, leadership and finances. Then we leaders return home and contextualize what we have learned to our cultures and the specific needs of our ministries.

We took seriously Paul's advice in 2 Corinthians: "taking precaution that no one should discredit us in our administration of this generous gift, for we have regard for what is honorable, not only in the sight of the Lord but also in the sight of men." We knew that being accountable to the Lord was vital to the ministry of Potter's House.

Another milestone came in 2003 when we had our first financial audit. Guatemala does not require audits for nonprofits, but for us, it was a way to demonstrate that we were being good stewards of the resources with which God had entrusted us. Then, in 2005, the Lord opened the door for the creation of Potter's House Association International as a U.S. 501(c)(3) nonprofit organization. And in 2009, we were accredited by the Evangelical Council for Financial Accountability (ECFA). None of these processes was easy, but we knew they were important steps in building the financial credibility and accountability we needed to raise funds to support the work of the ministry.

What Does Potter's House Do?

By 2020, Edgar had become such a committed member of the CLA that he was asked to chair that year's Outcomes Conference. Commenting on the challenges of ministry in an article titled "I Just Wanted to Serve the Poor," Edgar explained that love and passion are not enough to accomplish God's work. He shared what we had learned over the years as we prepared ourselves to lead the ministry in the following areas:

1. Programs and services for beneficiaries.
2. Relationships with donors and volunteers.
3. Support services, internal processes and systems.
4. Direction and leadership.
5. Governance and Board.

God helped us take the next step, and we started to formalize the structure of the ministry. Previously, it had been difficult to answer the simple question: What does Potter's House do? As we focused on the answer to that question, the Lord led us to some important conclusions.

Who We Are

Potter's House is a Christian non-profit organization that for more than 30 years has been working with the scavenger families of the garbage dump in Guatemala City. Even though they live, work, and often find their food in the garbage, they are not trash. They

Even though they live, work, and often find their food in the garbage, they are not trash.

are human beings with value and dignity. To God and to us, they are Treasures—determined, hard-working people.

Vision. One day not even one Treasure will scavenge in all of beautiful Guatemala.

Mission. To provide holistic opportunities for scavenger families by equipping them to be able to develop and transform their lives, families, and community.

Purpose. To love God, establish His Kingdom, and act for His glory. To love our neighbors as ourselves by valuing the Scavengers as Treasures through our love and service.

We defined our objectives as:

Assistance. To offer humanitarian aid and assistance to those who cannot help themselves, especially children and the elderly.

Development. To equip the Treasures to develop themselves and become confident, competent, and self-sustaining.

Empowerment. To provide resources with which the Treasures can participate in the solution of their personal, family, community, and national problems.

How We Work

Once we knew who we were, we were able to focus on the structure that would help us accomplish our vision, mission, and objectives.

The first thing we did was to create five programs to help the Treasures find opportunities for life beyond the garbage.

1. **Personal Development Program.** We empower the Treasures by giving them opportunities to develop leadership skills and encouraging their participation in finding solutions to community problems. We do this by training and supporting leaders and offering opportunities for the Treasures to receive practical Christian guidance for life.

2. **Education Program.** We holistically equip and shape the lives of the Treasures from elementary school through university. We teach them, in addition to academic subjects, Christian principles and values. We do this through after-school enrichment activities for our little Treasures and parenting classes for their families.

3. **Health Program.** We provide medical care for the Treasures, treating their minor illnesses and supporting them when serious illness strikes. In addition, we educate them in the basics of disease prevention and personal hygiene. We do this through medical clinics staffed by local doctors and international volunteers.

We provide financial resources and guidance to small businesses owners.

4. **Micro-Enterprise Program.** We provide financial resources and guidance to small businesses owners. This support enables them to grow

their small businesses, increase their income and improve their lives and the lives of their families. We do this through training in good business practices, assessment of project potential, small loans and oversight of accountability groups.

5. **Community Support Program**. We support the Treasures during especially difficult times when they cannot help themselves. We do this through the Nutrition Program, which provides a hot meal each school day for the children in our Education Program and distribution of bags of food, clothing, and other necessities when we see a need. We also respond immediately to emergencies such as fires, earthquakes, floods and other natural disasters. In addition, the community projects—new homes, concrete floors, sidewalks, walls, etc.—done by our volunteers are part of the Community Support Program.

As we sought to implement those programs, we developed the four-step process shown in Figure 1, which was designed to help us remember that our mission was not simply to hand out resources. We believed in the capacity of the Treasures, and we wanted to help them change from the inside out, demonstrating that change starts with a person's spirit, mind, will and emotions.

Step 1:	I do it	You learn
Step 2:	I do it	You help
Step 3:	You do it	I help
Step 4:	You do it	I support

Figure 1. The Four-Step Process.

The Lord led us to build a new community. Lives were being shaped by the Potter's hands. The Treasures were learning to build better relationships, helping and supporting one another as they worked to overcome the limitations and challenges that would otherwise defeat them. God transformed them into a new community. We saw influential leaders, better neighbors, better parents, happy children, and lots of hopes and dreams for the future.

Community Leadership

In January 2002, Potter's House started working with 100 leaders in the garbage dump community—several from each of the neighborhoods in the area. We didn't want to be seen as the solvers of their problems or the wealthy know-it-alls telling the Treasures what to do, so we worked with these community representatives to develop their leadership skills and empower them to be the voice of the people in their neighborhoods.

We didn't want to be seen as the solvers of their problems or the wealthy know-it-alls telling the Treasures what to do.

It was a novel concept, but the leaders soon grasped the importance of their role and began to make proposals and solve problems to better their communities and their lives. Among their initiatives were projects that have been undertaken to ensure better law enforcement and eradicate child labor in the dump. Potter's House also relies on the community leaders when volunteer teams come to build concrete-block homes for the Treasures. Potter's House has criteria that must be met by the beneficiaries, but it is the leaders who choose the families who will receive the homes. They also explain the criteria to help lessen the inevitable jealousy among neighbors.

One of the important lessons I have learned is that I am a steward not an owner of the ministry. R. Scott Rodin, a Christian writer and expert on stewardship and leadership development, suggests that we start by defining a *steward leader*. He tells us that "a steward leader is a faithful steward who has been called to lead." He goes on to say that it is important to identify the mindset of a prospective leader, which we can do by considering the attitudes listed in Figure 2.

Owner Mindset	Steward Mindset
The meaning of life is found within me, I need nothing else but me.	The meaning in life is found in Jesus, and I find it when I surrender my life to Him.
My choices are my own and no one should criticize them.	Our life, and our choices are not our own, and we must be stewards of our relationships with others, even if it means challenging the choices they make.
Fulfillment comes in pursuing the things I desire. I own my life, and I am the center of determining what is good and fulfilling for me.	Fulfillment comes from surrendering ourselves in love and service to others. God determines what is fulfilling for me, because my life belongs to Him.
I control my life, so I pursue those things which bring me pleasure. Pleasure is my measurement for success.	God controls my life, so I pursue those things which bring Him glory. His glory is my definition of success.
My life is mine, so if you want to believe something I disagree with, that's fine; just make sure it does not interfere with my own pursuit of happiness.	My life is God's and when He calls me to live and act and speak His truth, I will do so understanding it will upset, offend and disturb some people. This is not my intent, but I will be faithful regardless of the cost.
My ideas of sexual expression are mine alone, and no one has the right to tell me or anyone else to live any other way.	Our sexuality and the boundaries of its expression belong to God, and we follow and advocate for His ways as faithful steward

Figure 2. The attitudes of owners and stewards. Used with permission.

Recognition

For God's glory in August 2002, Potter's House Association won a second-place award and received a grant from the Juan Bautista Gutierrez Foundation, one of the most respected foundations in Guatemala. The contest, called "Supporting those Who Support," was created to recognize organizations involved in offering social development and assistance. One hundred and twenty-eight national organizations applied for this prize.

To qualify, the organization had to meet specific criteria, within the following areas: populations and range of action, kind of programs and services, stability and terms of service, resources invested in the community, efficiency and administrative capacity, volunteer participation, and board participation.

This award was unique because it originated from our home country—Guatemala—and it has served to open the eyes of many more Guatemalans to the "Treasures" in our backyard.

In April 2014, PHA received the 2013 Norman Borlaug Humanitarian Award. The nomination was presented by MedAssets, an American healthcare performance improvement company. Our name was submitted to MedAssets by Marilyn Monasterio, a MedAssets employee who with her husband Antonio spent a year volunteering at Potter's House in 2008.

Edgar, my husband, had the privilege of being the executive director of Potter's House Guatemala for 15 years and co-founder of Potter's House International and its director for 12 years. Together, we served for a total of 25 years. Then Edgar received a new call from the Lord. He felt that he had accomplished the work God had given him at Potter's House, so, in 2016, he delegated his responsibilities to the next generation of leaders so he could launch a new ministry. Edgar was part of the second generation; now the third and fourth generation of servant leaders continues God's ministry at Potter's House.

I Just Wanted to Serve the Poor

All I ever wanted was to serve our Treasures in the name of Jesus with all my heart. I had no idea it would be so complicated to achieve what seemed such a simple goal.

> *All I ever wanted was to serve our Treasures in the name of Jesus with all my heart.*

Following God's will and guiding PHA in the midst of a constantly changing environment—nationally and internationally—has been very stressful! We could never have done it alone.

In 2016, in the context of PHA's 30th anniversary, many friends, American missionaries, and colleagues from other Latin ministries asked us: How has PHA been able to survive for 30 years?

Every time we have faced with a problem or a complicated decision, we turn to the Lord our God for guidance. We also rely on a National Board of Directors, an International Board, and leaders from among our Guatemalan staff who are extremely capable and committed to the Lord.

Sometimes we expect that God will answer us with money. But He has taught me that being our Provider can mean many things. He will always provide, but the provision may be training, books, advisers and, yes, many times money.

Even our human gifts and talents are given in God's Grace. What a privilege, then, when He invites us to collaborate with Him to achieve His plans and *Eternal* purposes.

At Potter's House, we believe that what we do is follow God's will.

It was essential for me to understand that I am not an owner of what He has entrusted to me. I am just a steward; it all belongs to God.

Our Father, in heaven, hallowed be your name,
and your kingdom come, your will be done on
earth as it is in heaven.—**Matthew 6:9-10**

Personal or Group Follow-Up

What misconceptions might you have regarding "fund raising"?

↪

What does it mean to you to foster an "exchange of blessings" with your support team?

↪

What steps are you taking to continue learning from others?

↪

In your everyday experience, to whom do you turn when you are faced with a problem or complicated decision?

Additional Resources

For more information about the Christian Leadership Alliance (CLA) and the services they offer, visit their website: christianleadershipalliance.org

For more information about the Global Trust Partners (GTP) and the services they offer, visit their website: gtp.org

The Sower: Redefining the Ministry of Raising Kingdom Resources. Scott Rodin and Gary Hoag. ECFA Press. 2010.

The Choice: The Christ-Centered Pursuit of Kingdom Outcomes. Gary Hoag, H. R. Scott Rodin, and Wesley K. Willmer. ECFA Press. 2014.

The Council: A Biblical Perspective on Board Governance. Gary Hoag, Wesley K. Willmer, and Gregory J. Henson. ECFA Press. 2018.

CHAPTER 15

An Unexpected Blessing

Volunteers have played a vital role in the history of Potter's House. Beginning with the two Guatemalan co-founders, almost all the work of Potter's House was done by volunteers. Many members of the staff started as volunteers, and some of them are still part of the team years later.

After several years, word of Potter's House started to spread among international (mostly North American) friends who heard about the ministry and wanted to help.

Working with another culture was very challenging in the beginning. Volunteers with good intentions wanted to solve our problems, and many ended up doing more harm than good. In 1993, we had a particularly bad experiences with young international volunteers and made the difficult decision not to accept any more volunteers for a while. Then Dr. John Curlin, whom we had met several years earlier, wrote to us saying that he thought Potter's House would be the perfect place for his son Farr to work as a volunteer before going on to medical school.

Farr Remembers

Farr Curlin recalls his experience:

> Sometime in March of 1993 I called Dr. Lucrecia de Hernandez at her home in Guatemala City. My father had met "Dr. Lucky"' two years earlier, when a friend had

encouraged him to visit a rag-tag ministry led by three courageous women on the edge of the Guatemala City garbage dump (the *basurero*, as it was called). I asked Dr. Lucky if I could spend the upcoming year working with these women at Potter's House. In a moment of weakness, she consented but told me clearly, "We do not have time to babysit. If you want to work, you figure out how to get here and where to live."

> *We do not have time to babysit. If you want to work, you figure out how to get here and where to live.*

So I entered on the most consequential year of my life. I remember my first day at Potter's House. I walked the mile from the place where I had found a room through the streets of Guatemala City toward the *basurero*. The sweet, sickly smell of rotting garbage steadily grew, as concrete streets gave way to dirt and a fog of dust. I had made a map to follow, but I didn't need it. I could simply take my directions from the hundreds (thousands?) of buzzards circling over the dump. At my destination I found a wall of recycled barrels on wooden posts, with a crude gate secured by wire. *Casa del Alfarero* read the sign.

Inside I found a dirt floor enclosure with a whirlwind of activity. At one end a score of children surrounded "Seño Gladys," entreating her for some kind of treat as she laughingly led them toward the lunch line. In another corner, Lisbeth Piedrasanta was talking animatedly to some adult *guajeros* (recyclers), from whom she turned to greet me. Within minutes she had given me a long list of things she wanted me to work on. Dr. Lucky was in the *clínica*, examining several patients. Within moments Dr. Lucky told me to join her on a house call.

We went around the corner, down mud paths with human sewage flowing in little ruts, to a square room recently constructed by volunteers. There lay our patient, Don Lorenzo, a middle-aged man with alcoholism whose leg had been run over by a garbage truck after he had passed out on a curb. A surgery had left him with a number of steel pins sticking through his leg, and the wounds were getting infected. We picked up Don Lorenzo and put him in a crude wheelchair, then into Dr. Lucky's little car for a trip to the public hospital, where I waited with him for hours seeking attention. To no avail. We returned him to the "house" where he lived until we were able to arrange an amputation for him. He died a few months later.

So I was introduced to the complexity of what Potter's House teaches as the Eight Forms of Poverty. In Lorenzo Lopez, I found Poverty of the Will, Poverty of Affection, Poverty of Education, Financial Poverty, Physical Poverty, and more. At the same time, I was introduced to the Potter's House Way, established by these women at the outset: solidarity with the Treasures; patience; dogged and unflagging efforts to befriend, encourage, support, and heal in Christ's name; and perseverance undergirded by the experience of God providing enough for each day, usually one day at a time.

> *I was introduced to the complexity of what Potter's House teaches as the Eight Forms of Poverty.*

My entire grasp of what it means to be a Christian was turned upside down that year. I came with a well-managed spiritual life, clear goals, and plenty of intellectual knowledge. At Potter's House I confronted Christ among those who are poor, making demands on me that I resented—demands to relinquish being in control, and to love others without keeping an account.

In Gladys, Lisbeth, and Lucky, and later in Edgar Güitz and Joshua Jagelman, a Potter's House servant who came to be one of my closest friends, I found people surrendering to Christ in these ways. Exposed for what I was—a half-hearted and double-minded man—I first wanted to get away, but my soul longed for the life they had found, and by God's grace I stayed on and learned some of what our Lord had been teaching them. I will be forever grateful.

Still today, we celebrate with joy our work together. Farr became a physician and shared Potter's House with his family and friends. Later, he served as a member and then chairman of the PHA International Board of Directors. Today, Farr A. Curlin, M.D., is Josiah C. Trent Professor of Medical Humanities at the Trent Center for Bioethics, Humanities and History of Medicine, and Co-Director of the Theology, Medicine and Culture Initiative at Duke University Divinity School.

Farr restored our faith in international volunteers. He helped us deal with another culture that we did not understand and that did not understand us. We decided to reconsider the no-volunteers policy, and now, a quarter of a century later, we rejoice in the thousands of volunteers from Guatemala, the United States and other parts of the world who have served the Treasures of the garbage dump.

Like Farr, many others who have come as volunteers have seen God transform their lives.

Like Farr, many others who have come as volunteers have seen God transform their lives. Some have come struggling with problems in their own lives and as they have served the Treasures have found the Lord in a very unexpected place. Adults, teenagers, and children; Guatemalans, North Americans, Europeans, Asians, and Australians—volunteers of all ages and many nationalities have served here. They all saw in this ministry an opportunity to share the love of God and extend a hand to the needy. Some of them have even become full-time missionaries.

Volunteers Get Another Chance

After spending a year with Farr, we "three courageous women" decided to give volunteers another chance, but we knew we had to create a more structured experience for them. Our goal was to offer deeply meaningful opportunities that would allow volunteers to enrich the lives of the Treasures as well as their own. We wanted to help volunteers gain a personal knowledge of poverty and develop a love for the people who are afflicted by it.

To that end, over the years, Potter's House has developed and now offers four mission trip options to provide meaningful experiences for volunteers of all ages and interests. These are described in Appendix A.

We have come a long way since the day Farr Curlin walked into our little shack on the edge of the dump. Our volunteer program is well-structured and well-organized thanks to the work of our staff and their dedication to Jesus' example of service to the poor. This chapter is dedicated to all the volunteers who have come to serve the Treasures in the name of Jesus. Some served for years, some for weeks or days, but to all of them, we are forever grateful. Their legacy in the garbage dump community lives on and will never be forgotten.

*Those who cry as they plant crops will sing
at harvest time. Those who cry as they carry
out the seeds will return singing and carrying
bundles of grain.*—**Psalm 125:5-6 (EXB)**

Personal or Group Follow-Up

What are some of the blessings and challenges you
have faced in working either with volunteers or as
a volunteer?

●

In what ways could you relate to Farr Curlin's
story?

●

What steps are you taking to use volunteerism as
an opportunity to learn about poverty?

CHAPTER 16

An Exchange of Blessings

"Thank you for saving my marriage! We were about to get a divorce, but after my husband went to serve the Treasures, he changed."

My husband, Edgar, and I were visiting friends in the U.S., and one morning after we had shared about God's work among the Treasures in a church, a woman came to us with that touching story of a marriage redeemed. It surprised us; we didn't know they had problems. But God knew and eventually called that man and his wife to full-time ministry in Colombia.

That grateful wife was not alone; many people came to us wanting to tell us how God was transforming their lives through the ministry. We were amazed and surprised. We had never considered that the work volunteers did in the garbage dump community would change their lives as well as the lives of the Treasures.

We also heard reports of volunteers professing faith in Christ for the first time and the dynamics of entire families being changed for the better as parents and kids alike became aware of how privileged they were and how God was meeting the many needs of the Treasures.

We realized that God was fulfilling His promises, moving in and transforming the hearts of His people. The Bible has promises for those who serve the poor. Jesus affirmed that when we serve the poor, we will not lose our reward, and God will receive the glory. Jesus said even a gesture as small as giving a cup of cold water is service in His eyes, and when we serve, we receive His blessing. We also honor Him. As it says in Proverbs 14:31, "Whoever oppresses the poor shows contempt for their Maker, but whoever is kind to the needy honors God."

The testimonies of some of the people whose lives were changed in the garbage dump community follow. Praise Him!

A Couple Transformed

It is difficult to talk about just one of them. So, we always talk about Jim and Ruth Youngsman together, partners in life now for over 58 years. We have observed this pattern in their adventures: they are always together.

During their marriage, Jim and Ruth have quietly planted seeds as role models and partners in life, fighting battles together, experiencing common adventures, enjoying life, and loving each other. When Ruth was diagnosed with cancer many years ago, Jim said, "Ruth alone is not sick; we both are sick. We are fighting cancer together." By God's grace, they won that battle.

In 1987, Jim and Ruth heard the story of our work among the people living in the garbage dump of Guatemala City when Lisbeth spoke at the home of one of their friends in their hometown in Washington state. The ministry was in its infancy. It had no history, no financial backing, and no structure. It didn't even have a name. The story Lisbeth told was about two women just doing a favor at Christmas time, sharing 350 blankets in the name of Jesus.

Maybe it was Jim's business instinct that tempted him to get involved in this risky fledgling ministry.

Maybe it was Jim's business instinct that tempted him to get involved in this risky fledgling ministry. Only God knows why Jim and Ruth faithfully supported Potter's House financially for more than three decades. During that time, they helped us create our first slogan: "Valuing the Scavengers as Treasures."

Then in 1997, they took a leap of faith and turned their ongoing support into a personal friendship. They traveled to Guatemala to see the ministry first hand. From that first visit until today, Jim and Ruth have opened their hearts and shared with us what they have learned through their experiences as Christians, husband and wife, businesspeople, and parents.

They have also been a window on the world, helping us to have a global perspective. They encourage us to listen to God through prayer, not to take life too seriously, and to enjoy life and God's creation.

They have returned to Guatemala many times to share their expertise. Jim has mentored the PHA staff and clients of the Micro-Enterprise Program. Ruth has prayed for the staff and with hundreds of Treasures, who have found comfort amid their suffering through their prayer time with her. Together, they have led workshops on parenting, business, healthy eating, and the Christian life.

Together, they have led workshops on parenting, business, healthy eating, and the Christian life.

I hope that Jim and Ruth are happy they took a chance on that fledgling organization. After 33 years of involvement, they can see that the seeds they planted have grown into a forest in which thousands of people have served. They have encouraged us to overcome our fears and take bold steps in trusting God.

One of their own bold steps was sponsoring 15 young Treasures in our Education Program, all of whom view Jim and Ruth as their American grandparents. All 15 of them have finished school, and two of them have graduated from universities in the United States thanks to the Walton International Scholarship Program.

With Jim and Ruth's endorsement and involvement, in 2005, Potter's House Association International became a 501(c)(3) nonprofit organization in the United States with an office in Waukesha, Wisconsin. By unanimous vote, Jim was named the first chairperson and Ruth a member of the first board of directors of the ministry. The Youngsmans took a chance on a couple of blanket-delivering young women who were trusting the Lord, and I know they believe their investment has been repaid many times over.

A Family Transformed

The journey of Paul and Nancy Mullen and their three daughters began in 1998. Paul tells their story:

> We were part of what we now call a vision trip. Our youngest daughter, Carrie, was just two-years old at the time. Our regular engagement over the years as PHA volunteers became pivotal for the formation of our family. Our daughters came to see international service as a part of ordinary life. Potter's House was important enough to our second daughter, Julie, that a visit to PHA was a prerequisite for marriage to her husband who had not yet known the ministry.
>
> As adults, we have learned many things about serving well through our engagement with the Potter's House staff, volunteers, and Treasures. When Gladys asked me to write

about our involvement with PHA, I came up with several thoughts, which I discuss here in no particular order.

The word "Treasures," as a replacement for *scavengers* or *beneficiaries* was a monumentally important change of both mindset and language. At the time, I found the phrasing to be problematic because it did not convey the depth of the need to donors. What I missed was the importance of the word in changing our posture of ministry. It was not so much that people in need got things that they needed but that people of value could be endowed with the necessities that allowed them to live in the dignity of that value. The Potter's House leadership saw this important difference early on.

The concept of Eight Forms of Poverty, which is discussed in Chapters 9 and 10, broadened our thinking about service. I have frequently commented to others, when explaining the Eight Forms of Poverty, that seven of the eight require physical presence. To be incarnational in the ministry, we need to either show up or enable others to show up.

We learned through practice and example that sometimes a gift comes with a burden.

We would often part ways after a time together, arguing about who had been more blessed by the experience over the preceding days. We adopted the phrase, "It has been an exchange of blessings." That became part of my regular storehouse of useful phrases, and I've used it many times. It illustrates the character of Christian community that is so attractive to those who take the time to look. This concept of Christian community as an exchange of blessings first got its voice at Potter's House.

We learned through the years of the need to ask permission to give. We learned through practice and example that sometimes a gift comes with a burden. There's a long-told allegory of the gift of a white elephant, which though special, requires uncommon care and expense. We have learned that beyond trivial giving, true generosity requires either an intimacy that understands the burden of gift or the overt question, "Would this be a welcome gift?

Our first visit to Guatemala was a vision trip. But our interaction with Potter's House over the years has broadened our vision of the specifics of the ministry and improved our ability to see, appreciate and incorporate the vision of others around the world.

Paul and Nancy Mullen have brought technological skills and expertise in many other areas to help the ministry grow. Paul has served as part of the International Board of Directors, and they have been running the office of Potter's House International in the United States since 2005. We praise God for the Mullens.

A Church Transformed

Mendham Hills Community Church of the Christian & Missionary Alliance is a thriving evangelical church located in Mendham, New Jersey.

The Lord sent a team from Mendham to Potter's House for the first time in 2005. Since then, they have partnered with us in planting seeds of love in many ways. We are taught in Mark 4:24-27 that "God's kingdom is like seed thrown on a field by a man who then goes to bed and forgets about it. The seed sprouts and grows—he has no idea how it happens." (MSG)

Their love for the Lord, their friendship, their commitment, and their love for the Treasures have extended His Kingdom in Guatemala. Here is their story in the words of John Isemann, pastor of the church.

It was January 2005, and my alma mater, Rutgers University, was making a very rare appearance in a bowl game, so my brothers and I went to ESPN Zone in New York City to watch the game.

As we made our way along the cold, crowded sidewalk, I noticed a homeless man with hand outstretched begging for money. I reached into my pocket, searching for a small bill to give him, but I found only a twenty-dollar bill—much too much to give a beggar—so I pulled my hand out of my pocket and kept walking. I hadn't gone more than a few steps when I felt God telling me to give the guy my twenty, so I went back and placed the bill in the man's empty cup.

I quickly caught up with my family, eager to share my good deed. "Did you see that homeless guy back there? I gave him a twenty!" The theme continued through the evening and throughout the following week; I missed no opportunity to tell anyone who would listen—my wife, my staff, my friends, and even a few strangers—what a great guy I was.

> *I missed no opportunity to tell anyone who would listen—my wife, my staff, my friends, and even a few strangers—what a great guy I was.*

God, however, was not as impressed; I was convicted when I heard Him tell me, "You have already received your reward."

Shortly thereafter, I was sitting, talking with some friends, and the subject of poverty came up. I said to my friends,

"You know, I don't really care about the poor."

"Yes, you do," they responded. "You're a pastor; of course, you care about the poor."

"No, I don't," I said. "I'm sorry they're poor, but I don't care enough to do anything about it." I was convicted again and knew I had to do something about my lack of interest in the people that Christ loved and often chose to spend His time with.

At about the same time, one of the national news magazines published a list of the 200 wealthiest communities in the United States, and Mendham, New Jersey, the town in which my church is located was on that list. When I saw that, I knew that as the pastor of the church I had to do something to change the hearts of my people—something to help them move beyond the bubble in which they lived.

We were a Christian & *Missionary* Alliance church that had never offered a mission trip to our congregation. I was determined to change that. I started with the C&MA and learned that they had nothing available, because February was too late to start planning a summer trip.

Undaunted, I asked the head of our Missions Team to find a place very different from Mendham to which we could send a team that summer. A month or so later, he reported that he had found a ministry in Haiti that needed volunteers. Unfortunately, he also found that there was a ban on travel to Haiti by U.S. citizens. He also found a place called Potter's House that served the people who depended on the Guatemala City garbage dump for their livelihoods.

I told him to start planning a trip to Potter's House, but I added what I felt was an important restriction: I knew no one would be willing to take an entire week of vacation to work in a garbage dump, so I set a limit of three workdays for the trip. That way we could be reasonably certain to enlist a few intrepid souls for our church's first mission trip.

In fact, 26 intrepid souls signed up for the trip. I remember standing with my wife in our kitchen at 3:30 a.m. on the morning of departure. "What are we doing?" I asked her. "We're leaving our four kids behind so we can work in a garbage dump. Are we crazy?"

"We're leaving our four kids behind so we can work in a garbage dump. Are we crazy?"

Apparently, we were, because we headed to not-very-nearby JFK airport and flew with our team to a country none of us had ever visited. Our two projects were to pour concrete floors in three shacks in the community surrounding the dump and paint the bare cinder-block walls of a huge, four-story-high dining room/gym/auditorium at Potter's House.

I was proud of the way our team pitched in and worked in that filthy, foul-smelling environment. By the second day, they were making plans to return the following year. I was not going to be able to check "mission trip" off my list and move on. My people were hooked, and soon, so was I.

Three things stand out in my mind when I think of that first trip. The first was a little girl washing a cut on her foot in a puddle of filthy water. The second was the swarm of kids playing soccer on the "streets" of the community where we were working. They were having a fantastic time with nothing more than a battered soccer ball. My third memory is of being introduced to one of the Treasures—a man about my own age. I held out my hand to shake his, and he snatched his hand away, hanging his head to indicate he felt unworthy to shake my hand. My heart ached for him.

Two years later, as more and more people wanted to go the Potter's House, we formed a secular nonprofit organization to run trips to PHA. We wanted to be able to attract people from our community who did not go to our church—or perhaps, any church—and we wanted to be able to accept donations and matching funds from corporations that would not donate to a church. That organization is called Beyond the Walls, and 14 years later, we send about 150 volunteers a year to Potter's House—three back-to-back weeks in the summer and another week in the fall or spring. Those volunteers come from 15 states, so we have definitely branched out beyond the walls of Mendham Hills Community Church.

But, to me, the most important result of our involvement with Potter's House has been the change it has made in our congregation. As we learned to look outward—to focus on things beyond our walls rather than activities to serve ourselves—the entire culture of the church changed.

About half of our congregation has been to Potter's House, and the majority of those return year after year. Going to Guatemala has become a regular part of many families' lives. Children long for their 13th birthdays so they can go to Potter's House. Just about every family that goes sponsors at least one child in the PHA Education Program [Appendix B], and they consider those kids part of their families. Spending time with them is a highlight of the summer. And those who can't go are generous in supporting those who can; no volunteer has ever had to cancel a trip due to lack of funds.

Children long for their 13th birthdays so they can go to Potter's House.

People have met Christ in that dump and turned their lives

over to Him. Students who worked in the garbage dump as teenagers have become adults who have gone into full-time ministry—both at home and abroad. Potter's House staff members have visited us for periods ranging from a couple days to six weeks, and we love them all.

We have also sent teams to an Indian Reservation in South Dakota, and our church staff gives up their offices for a week twice a year so we can host temporarily homeless families in the house where we work. Our volunteers provide food, companionship, and other support while those families are with us and often after they move into permanent housing.

During the Covid-19 pandemic, members of our congregation kept their eyes focused outward, providing food for those homeless families, meals for medical professionals at our hospital, and toys for hospitalized children. In addition, they offered substantial financial support to church members who had lost their jobs and suffered other setbacks. We have also sent substantial sums to our partners in Guatemala to feed the poor and pay their employees.

The guy who gave a beggar a twenty could never have imagined the impact that simple act would have on the lives of thousands of poor Guatemalans and middle-class Americans. We started out as most volunteers do, thinking we would change the lives of the people we served, but we soon realized that "The life you change could be your own!"

As these testimonies show, when we serve others, God transforms us in unexpected ways. We soon learned that transformation comes not only to the people served but to all of us. Together, we continue acting as the Body of Christ, sharing our talents, time, and treasure. Thousands of volunteers have contributed to the vision of seeing the Christ-life flourish in our Guatemala.

*And if anyone gives even a cup of cold water to
one of these little ones because he is my disciple,
I tell you the truth, he will certainly not lose his
reward.*—**Matthew 10:42**

Personal or Group Follow-Up

Pastor John Isemann warns that when you
volunteer, the "life you change could be your own."
In what ways have you seen God work in the lives
of those who come wanting to bless others but
find that they are the ones who have been blessed?

↬

Which of the three stories (a couple, a family or
a church) do you most relate to? How so?

Additional Resources

For more information about Mendham Hills Community Church,
visit their website: mendhamhills.org

For more information about 7 Standards of Excellence in Short Term
Mission, visit their website: soe.org

Jesus in me: Experiencing the Holy Spirit as a Constant Companion.
Anne Graham Lotz. Multnomah. 2019.

Experiencing God Together: God's Plan to Touch Your World.
Henry T. Blackaby and Melvin D. Blackaby. Broadman & Holman
Publishers, 2002.

CHAPTER 17

Following God's Will for His Glory

People sometimes say to me, "Gladys, after 34 years of service, you must be happy that all your dreams for the ministry have come true." I laugh and answer, "I never planned any of this."

The ministry God entrusts to us as leaders is not ours; we are just stewards, and our knowledge must be shared with others who are trustworthy and reliable and, therefore, qualified to teach others.

As I mentioned in Chapter 14, Scott Rodin, a Christian writer and expert on stewardship and leadership development, helps us to understand both of those areas better with the six fundamental questions shown in Figure 1.

I didn't have the benefit of Scott's teaching at the time, but I did come to realize that the ministry was not mine. Acquiring the steward mindset about the ministry that He had entrusted to me, released me from many burdens I carried when I thought the ministry was dependent on me.

I remember how difficult it was for me when staff members left the PHA team to work with other organizations. We had invested time, training, and resources in them, and then they left us. It was not fair! Sometimes it even made me angry.

Then one day God opened my eyes. "They are mine, not yours," He told me.

I realized how important it was to join the Lord in equipping a new generation to work wherever He could use them to build His Kingdom.

"You are investing in my people and my Kingdom. You are preparing them to take on my next challenge." Ouch! It was a painful lesson. At the same time, I realized how important it was to join the Lord in equipping a new generation to work wherever He could use them to build His Kingdom.

What a difference that realization made! God was inviting people to serve at Potter's House, and it was our job to recruit, nurture, and train them to do His work—wherever He called them. Of course, it was still painful every time I heard that a member of our staff was moving on, but I viewed the transition differently once I learned to thank them for serving at PHA. Then I could send them off with blessings and prayer that they would flourish in another place for His glory and His kingdom.

Fundamentals	Ownership Mindset	Steward Mindset
Security Who do I trust?	I trust myself, therefore I do not rest. I wonder if I am good enough.	I trust God and Christ. I rest in His sufficiency.
Identity Who am I?	I am the owner of my identity. The Life of Christ is secondary.	I am an image bearer. I am a child of God.
Belonging Who wants me?	I establish my own kingdom. I strive to protect my empire.	I belong to Christ's Kingdom.
Purpose Why I am here?	I seek my own purpose.	God has a purpose. I have an assignment.
Outcomes What difference can I make?	I own my impact and results.	I leave results to God.
Competence What am I good at?	I demand perfection. I depend on my own strengths and strategies.	I depend on God gifts and giftedness.

Figure 1. Ownership vs. Stewardship. Used with permission.

One Who Stayed

The first big gathering we had was held in the church near the garbage dump in 1987. The Lord called a group of hard-working Guatemalan volunteers to help with that first event, and everything was planned for 1,000 people—500 children and 500 adults. I was nervous and excited. Everything was new; I knew only that I had to expect the unexpected. It was the first time any of us had participated in an event like this. We didn't know exactly what to do, so we asked God to lead us.

Three days before the event, we went to the dump to invite our guests. We decided to paint the index finger of each invitee as a way to identify the guests. A friend who was a biological chemist created, just for the occasion, a semi-permanent ink that would last for several days.

Long before the start time for the event, we were surprised to see that a long line had formed in front of the church. Our guests were eager to join the celebration. The Lord provided 1,000 tamales, our typical celebration food; 1,000 blankets; and 1,000 gifts. The plan was for the church pastor to share the gospel, and others to lead programs for kids and adults.

I thought to myself, "this boy looks very timid; I'm afraid these children will harm him."

As the volunteers arrived, I greeted Letty, her daughter, Marisol, and her 11-year old son, Héctor Rivas. Letty asked me to allow Héctor, to oversee 25 kids. I thought to myself, "this boy looks very timid; I'm afraid these children will harm him."

When I told Letty my concern, she replied, "Don't worry; he can handle it." Trusting in her mother's instinct, I assigned a group of 25 wild, active kids to Héctor, who immediately took charge and began to lead them. I was surprised, but God was not.

That was the beginning of our friendship with Héctor. A very responsible boy, he wanted to help us follow up with the kids at our Saturday programs. This time I didn't hesitate. I knew that if I gave him a job, he would do it well, as unto the Lord.

Héctor was a faithful servant, eventually leading the children's program on Saturdays. In 1994, when he finished high school at the age of 18, we invited him to join the Potter's House staff. The Lord had once again answered my prayer, sending another man for the team. Working with Héctor taught me that I did not have to consider the size or appearance of a volunteer; what was important was the person's heart.

Héctor grew up in a Christian family. His mother taught him to serve the poor, and he had been serving in his local church. Serving the Treasures opened his eyes as he realized that there was more to service than attending and helping out in the church.

Héctor worked side by side with us, taking on more responsibility over the years. After watching him work and lead for 16 years and prayerfully considering the future of Potter's House, my husband, Edgar, who was the executive director at that time, recommended to the board of directors that Héctor be named CEO of Potter's House Association Guatemala, a position he assumed on February 16, 2012.

Héctor has trusted God through numerous challenges along with the way. God has richly provided, and under his leadership, the work of Potter's House has flourished and expanded, taking advantage of the energy and dedication of the next generation, exploring new ways and new places to build God's Kingdom.

A Wife for Héctor

Part of the ministry that I have enjoyed over the years is watching members of our staff find their spouses at Potter's House, just as the Lord provided Edgar for me. Héctor met Margarita when they were both young volunteers. They married in 1999, and the Lord has blessed them with three daughters with whom they now serve the Treasures as a family.

Part of the ministry that I have enjoyed over the years is watching members of our staff find their spouses at Potter's House

Margarita started volunteering at the age of 15 when she served as a counselor for 6-year old girls at one of the camps. After finishing her elementary education training, she joined PHA as coordinator of the programs we offered for children and teenagers and later as director of the Family Integration Program. Because of her dedication to the well-being of those she serves, the Lord has entrusted her with several different positions at Potter's House, and she has become one of our key leaders.

God has been faithful. Through the years, he has guided us as we recruited, nurtured, and trained remarkable leaders and team members for the Potter's House staff.

The First Strategic Plan

In 2011, PHA leaders undertook the creation of our first strategic plan in an effort to ensure that the ministry would grow and flourish according to God's plan during the coming years.

Speaking of the first plan, Héctor says

We are thankful to God for the accomplishment of our strategic plan in 2019, which was yet another milestone in the ministry. We are witnesses of God's faithfulness and presence in the expansion of the ministry to other regions in the country and through innovative strategies to combat poverty.

He enabled us to systematize our Christ-centered model while we implemented the plans. The team is thankful to God for the transformation process we have experienced. We are very appreciative of having been invited to be a part of the expansion of His Kingdom in Guatemala.

This next stage, now that the ministry has a presence in three regions of the country, has required a new strategic plan. We are expectant! Once again, this has been a team effort; we have dedicated time to prayer, reflection, research and planning.

As part of our ongoing strategic plan [Appendix C], we want to honor God by proclaiming the good news to the needy as the primary means of transformation and strengthening of the ministry in the three regions of Guatemala. We pray for His guidance and presence. GOD HAS BEEN FAITHFUL.

If we believe that the ministry with which God has entrusted us is important to the growth of His Kingdom, we need to prepare successors who will guide the ministry when we are no longer able to do so. In 2 Timothy 2:2, we read, "You have heard me teach things that have been confirmed by many reliable witnesses. Now teach these truths to other trustworthy people who will be able to pass them on to others." (NLT)

As we prepare to celebrate the 35th anniversary of Potter's House, the Lord is expanding His Kingdom among the poor in Guatemala and continuing to transform the lives of staff, volunteers, and supporters who are part of the PHA family.

The religious life is static. The Christian life is *dynamic*. God continues moving people from religiosity to Christian life. It is a wonderful process: growing in Christ and experiencing God in unexpected places and surprising ways.

Potter's House has always been God's Idea, and He has sent a new generation to help execute it. God continues writing His story and calling us to do His work and follow His plans. I am grateful to God for the generation He has raised up and for allowing me by His grace to see it. God can do anything, you know—far more than you could ever imagine or guess or request in your wildest dreams!

Now to him who by his power within us is
able to do far more than we ever dare to ask
or imagine—to him be glory in the Church
through Jesus Christ for ever and ever, amen!
—Ephesians 3:20-21 (Phillips)

Personal or Group Follow-Up

In what ways do you struggle with having an owner mindset rather than a steward mindset? Which of those terms best describes your organization's culture?

↪

Who are some of the potential future leaders in your organization?

↪

How are you equipping others to be part of your succession plan?

Additional Resources

For more information about Potter's House Association Guatemala, visit our website: pottershouse.org.gt

The Steward Leader, Transforming People, Organizations and Communities. R. Scott Rodin. IVP Academic. 2013.

Lead Like Jesus: Lessons for Everyone from the Greatest Leadership Role Model of all Time. Ken Blanchard and Phil Hodges, Thomas Nelson. 2005

CHAPTER 18

The Most Wonderful Years of My Life!

"What was it like serving in the hostile environment of poverty for 30 years? How did you survive?"

I had been invited to share my experiences with a group of young ministry leaders, and that's what they wanted to know: how had I survived. Part of the answer is that, at the time, I was not completely aware of the struggle in which I was engaged. I felt that by God's grace I was answering His call. I was a living example of the believer Paul talks about in 2 Corinthians 3:5: "I am not saying that we can do this work by ourselves. It is God who makes us able to do all that we do."

Now, having survived those years, I often receive invitations to share the testimony of what God has done in my life. I enjoy telling that story because it is not my story; it is God's story in my life, and He will be glorified.

Many people tried to discourage me from doing what I thought God wanted me to do.

But it wasn't always like that. People told me I was crazy, that I was wasting my life and my education, that I would never find a husband. My doctor told me, "you are shortening your life. You will get lung cancer from the polluted environment." Many people tried to discourage me from doing what I thought God wanted me to do.

To serve 30 years in a row in a Latin ministry is a significant accomplishment. On December 24, 2021, Lord willing, we will celebrate our 35th anniversary, which is one of the reasons I am writing this book.

When I first went to the garbage dump and met the Treasures, I was afraid to follow Jesus into the unexpected places to which He was leading me. I didn't realize that He was leading me to a new life—a life in which I would move from religiosity to a vibrant Christian life. He would become my constant companion, guiding me every step of the way. During those 30 years, I have been getting to know Him better and learning that the places to which He leads us are the best places for us.

I have truly found God in unexpected places for His glory and for the expansion of His Kingdom. I see Him multiplying His servants and empowering them for His Kingdom, leading them from religiosity to Christian life just as He led me.

A Major Milestone

The year 2012 marked a milestone in the life of Potter's House. We celebrated 25 years of continuous service in the garbage dump of Guatemala City!

That year, I delegated the roles I had been filling at Potter's House to the next generation of leaders. But I did not retire. In my position as co-founder, I continue to be fully involved in the work of PHA in other capacities.

That year was also a milestone in my personal life. It was a year of transition that brought difficult adjustments in my life. I have since realized that during that time I was thinking about *doing* rather than *being*. I was the associate director of Potter's House, and my pride took a painful hit when I began to feel as if I was no longer useful. But in the end, I feel that "it is well with my soul." I have new freedom without the burdens that I had been carrying—the burdens that I originally lamented as losses.

Relinquishing the roles I had held for so many years felt like losing a child. The pain was tremendous. I asked God what plans He had for me in the years ahead. He answered me through Psalm 71, especially in verse 19:

Relinquishing the roles I had held for so many years felt like losing a child.

"*Tell the next generation, about His mighty acts and righteous deeds.*" At that moment, I did not completely understand how He wanted me to do that, but at least I knew He had a plan.

Covid Complications

As I write this, the Covid-19 pandemic is affecting the entire world, including Guatemala. The virus has made a poor country even poorer as we now see 67% percent of our population living in extreme poverty.

As a member of a vulnerable population because of my health and age, as much as I desperately wish I could, I cannot leave home and take my place at the forefront of serving the Treasures at this challenging time. It frustrates me, but this situation has been a good reminder that God still loves me even though I cannot be serving Him on the front lines of the battle against poverty.

But this experience has helped me to understand that the Lord has called me to share my knowledge and my story with the next generation in many ways. Praying, encouraging others, discipling others—and even writing this book—are my new ministries. And I am comfortable working from home, because I know that this is where God wants me to be. I don't need to be front-and-center in the ministry to accomplish His work. I can trust Him and see His provision right where I am.

Understanding my new role has changed my life yet again. My identity no longer comes from what I do, but rather from who I am because of Jesus Christ. God is more interested in who I am than in how much I can do. He continues to love me even though I can no longer serve Him 24/7. In Philippians 1:6, Paul tells us, "There has never been the slightest doubt in my mind that the God who started this great work in you would keep at it and bring it to a flourishing finish on the very day Christ Jesus appears."

One of my prayer requests has been that more Guatemalans would be moved to compassion and service, because I know that if we serve together as one family, our nation will be better. And although my country has a long way to go, I am grateful that the Lord has raised up a new generation of

I am grateful that the Lord has raised up a new generation of leaders at PHA that has taken my place on the front lines.

leaders at PHA that has taken my place on the front lines, serving the Treasures day-to-day and year-to-year. They are my heirs as surely as the biological children I never had would have been. It touches my heart to see those young Guatemalans serving in His name. Their dedication has created a new model of service, ministering to others not just at Christmas as was traditionally done, but all year long. They know that we are the permanent expression of God's love for the poor, exemplifying the truth of St. Teresa of Ávila's famous poem:

> *Christ has no body now but yours.*
>
> *No hands, no feet on earth but yours.*
>
> *Yours are the eyes through which he looks compassion on this world.*
>
> *Yours are the feet with which he walks to do good.*

Yours are the hands through which he blesses all the world.Yours are the hands, yours are the feet, yours are the eyes, and you are his body.

Christ has no body now on earth but yours.

Following Jesus has not been easy. Many times, I thought the challenges were too much for me, but I have learned to walk one day at a time, trusting in His promises.

The Power to Succeed

I have heard it said that with God's appointing comes God's anointing. That means that He never calls you to do something without providing the tools you need to do it. If He gives you an assignment, He will provide you with the Holy Spirit's help and empower you to complete it. We are reminded in Hebrews 13:20-21 that when the Lord calls us, He promises to walk with us: "Now may the God of peace—who brought up from the dead our Lord Jesus, the great Shepherd of the sheep, and ratified an eternal covenant with his blood—may he equip you with all you need for doing his will. May he produce in you, through the power of Jesus Christ, every good thing that is pleasing to him. All glory to him forever and ever! Amen." (NLT)

Even though I had been a Christian for a long time, I did not understand that concept when I was asked to do that "first favor" that became Potter's House. As I have walked with Him on this journey, I have learned that the power to succeed comes from Him. And as I relied on that power, I realized that the ministry was not mine; it was His.

We are taught to be self-sufficient, so it is easy to be tempted to rely on our strength when answering His call. I succumbed to that temptation many times, and eventually I learned that the inevitable result of trying to do God's will without His help is burnout.

The older I get, the more aware I become that it is not enough simply to receive God's call. How we live out that call and, ultimately, how we complete it are just as important. Finishing well transcends the specific calling because it becomes an example for those who come after us—the next generation. When they see what the Lord has enabled us to accomplish, they recognize the importance of the values by which we live.

The faith that enables us to prevail comes from the understanding that everything was created by God and for His purposes.

Over the years, I have learned that, although it is not always easy, it is ultimately satisfying and fulfilling to do everything as for the Lord. We need to set our eyes on Jesus and understand that everything we do should be for His glory. Then, we will live as Paul described in Acts 20:24: "But I do not pay any attention or value my life to myself, as long as I finish my career with joy, and the ministry that I received from the Lord Jesus, to bear witness to the gospel of the grace of God." (NKJV)

> *It is ultimately satisfying and fulfilling to do everything as for the Lord.*

I found God in some very unexpected places, and by His Grace, I experienced His presence as I served. I found my husband. I found contentment. I found significance. I learned and continue to learn new skills. I met celebrities. I experienced suffering. I found good friends. I found contentment. I saw miracles. I traveled to distant lands.

I have learned a lot from the poor; they have been my mentors. Working alongside them has made me feel alive. I learned to take my complaints directly to the Lord. I saw God providing resources to accomplish His purposes—often without money. And I learned not to take life for granted.

The Bible does not promise us that serving God will be easy or comfortable. We will find ourselves on dead-end streets, experiencing extreme uncertainty, and may even lose close friends. But with God, things meant for evil can be turned into good. As we read in Psalm 34:19, "The righteous person faces many troubles, but the Lord comes to the rescue each time."

From religiosity to Christian life. Thank you, Lord, for taking me beyond the walls of religion and leading me to a full Christian life.

For a long time, I thought my years at Potter's House were the most beautiful years of my life. And, indeed, they were. Nevertheless, I am now sensing that the most beautiful years of my life are yet to come. I do not want to limit God, as I did in the past. Now, my prayer is to respond as Mary, Jesus' mother did in Luke 1:38: "I am the Lord's servant. May your word to me be fulfilled."

You are blessed because you believed that the Lord would do what he said.—**Luke 1:15 (NLT)**

But whatever I am now, it is all because God poured out his special favor on me—and not without results.—**1 Corinthians 15:10a (NLT)**

Those who plant in tears will harvest with shouts of joy. They weep as they go to plant their seed, but they sing as they return with the harvest.—**Psalm 126:5-6 (NLT)**

They are planted in Yahweh's house.
They will flourish in our God's courts.
They will still bring forth fruit in old age.
—Psalm 92:13-14 (WEB)

Personal or Group Follow-Up

What are the hidden treasures God is inviting you to discover as you follow Him into unexpected places?

↝

In what ways do you wrestle with *doing* vs. *being*?

↝

How do you define your identity?

↝

What is the legacy you are building or leaving behind? How will it tell God's story and bring glory to Him?

Additional Resources

If you are interested in writing your own book, I recommend FlourishWriters (flourishwriters.com). FlourishWriters is a vibrant community of writers who desire to share their God stories.

Kisses from Katie: A Story of Relentless Love and Redemption.
Katie Davis. Howard Books. 2012.

Spiritual Leadership: Moving People on to God's Agenda.
Henry T. Blackaby and Richard Blackaby. B&H Books. 2011.

The Emotionally Healthy Church: A Strategy for Discipleship that Actually Changes Lives. Peter Scazzero. Zondervan. 2003.

The Purpose Driven Life: What on Earth am I Here for? Rick Warren.
Zondervan, 2002.

Miracles: God's Work in Pictures

Lisbeth (left) and me standing at the edge of the garbage dump with
some of the Treasures we were serving in 1993.

In 2015, a group of teenage Treasures who had grown up in Potter's House
programs went to serve other Treasures living around a garbage dump
in Chiquimula, a rural area about five hours from Guatemala City.

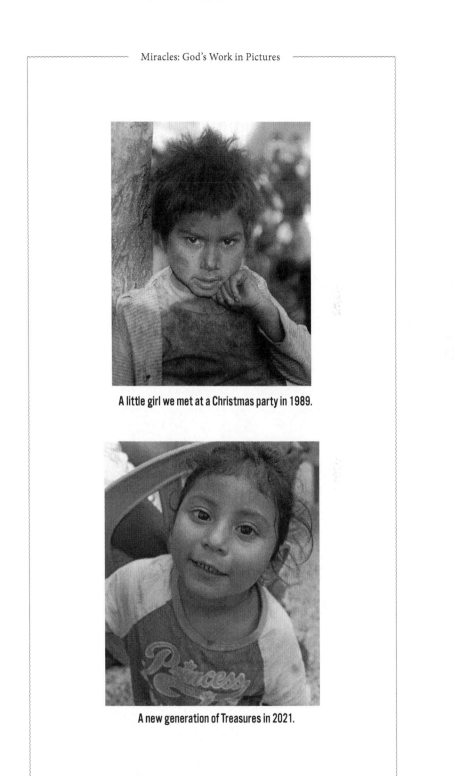

A little girl we met at a Christmas party in 1989.

A new generation of Treasures in 2021.

Our first building on the land we bought in 1993.

Our first medical clinic opened in 1993.

The new facility we built in 2004, after the fire.

The beginning of our Education Program (1993). We had no furniture, so the Treasures used concrete blocks for both tables and chairs.

When Potter's House was rebuilt after the fire, a temporary wooden structure was added for the Education Program. It was hot and dusty in those rooms, but the children had desks and other equipment and supplies.
So much better than concrete blocks!

In 2015, the third phase of expansion for the Education Program created large, bright classrooms for the Treasures.

The third phase of expansion also included colorful, well-equipped rooms for the younger Treasures.

A Treasure's Story: Kathy Rosales

Sweet baby. Kathy was only four-years old when she first came to Potter's House.

Fun is where you find it. Her playground was the garbage dump.

Family photo. Kathy (rear, second from left) with her mother and younger brother and sisters outside their home on the edge of the garbage dump.

Happy high school student. Kathy doing her homework in one of the classrooms at Potter's House.

College graduate. Kathy at her graduation from Harding University.

Proud mama. Kathy's mother Lorena was able to attend her graduation.

Bride and groom. Kathy and her husband Selvin leave their wedding.

Appendices

Appendix A

S.E.R.V.E. at Potter's House

Since its earliest days, Potter's House has worked alongside volunteers from Guatemala and around the world to build long-term relationships that will produce abundant fruit in the lives of the Treasures and volunteers alike.

God has allowed Potter's House to work alongside individuals, families, churches, businesses, organizations and foundations that participate in the work that God is doing in Guatemala by sharing their time, talent and treasure.

Our goal is to provide opportunities that promote an exchange of blessings and facilitate mutual transformation as we carry out the work that we have been called to do.

Through our S.E.R.V.E. program, Potter's House has hosted more than 7,000 volunteers over the past three decades. We call our volunteers "servants" for we encourage them to shift their mindset from one that volunteers to one that serves, like Jesus did.

There is still a lot of work to do and we are always looking for more partners and friends to join our mission so, if you are interested in serving along Potter's House individually, as a family, with your friends, church or business, contact us at: serve@pottershouse.org.gt.

Over the years, we have heard many of our servants say: *"Once you serve at Potter's House, your life will never be the same"* and we could not agree more! Will you join us?

Figure 1 shows how we describe the S.E.R.V.E. program, which makes that possible.

S	**Stewardship**. We are called to be good stewards of God's resources. We believe that every resource (time, tools, people) is provided by the Lord and with that in mind, we invite everybody that comes to serve with us to be an obedient steward of those resources.
E	**Excellence.** We want to imitate Jesus' quality of service. Because we are doing everything for God's glory, we motivate every person involved to do every project with the highest standards and at the same time, bring dignity to the Treasures (beneficiaries).
R	**Relationship-oriented.** We are people-oriented. Although there is a project that has to be done within a period of time, we believe encourage volunteers to build long-term relationships with the Treasures—at the expense project deadlines, if necessary. Projects are tools we use to enable us to spread the gospel among the people in the dump community.
V	**Versatile.** We need to be able to adapt and adjust to cultural differences and changing situations. There will always be a schedule and a plan, but things happen, and every volunteer needs to be flexible and open to change.
E	**Exchange.** When we serve others, we give and receive. We believe that God wants to bless all the participants in a given project and that He works among us through the Holy Spirit. We encourage each volunteer to listen for the special message that He will bless you with.

Want to get involved?

Our SERVE Program provides deep and meaningful opportunities for volunteers to enrich the lives of the Treasures as well as their own.

The groups we take are divided by type:

Short Term Missions

Intended for churches or organizations that want to expose individuals to the eye-opening experience of serving the poor. Participants will experience first-hand what God is doing in the communities.

Youth Mission Experience

This option gives your youth group an opportunity to participate in the adventure of serving the poor in an exciting and exotic place. It is a great way to help strengthen young adults' faith and character and change their perspective on life.

Family Mission Experience

Through this experience, a family can strengthen relationships between its members as you serve together in a Christian organization. Every member of the family can use their talents and abilities to share God's love with the poor.

All groups pay for their expenses in Guatemala and for the projects they do. PHA will provide a budget once plans are finalized.

For more information, contact serve@pottershouse.org.gt.

The Potter's House Sponsorship Program

With 17 million people, Guatemala has one of the largest populations in Central America.

According to UNICEF, 48% of the total population is under 18 years of age, and many of those children are at risk, facing malnutrition and the need to drop out of elementary school to care for younger siblings or to work in order to contribute to the family's income. These are the children and youth—we call them Treasures—that Potter's House seeks to impact through the Education Programs in our community centers.

Our Sponsorship Program is unique in that sponsors are always welcome to visit the children they sponsor at Potter's House.

When you sponsor a child, you help facilitate his or her physical, mental, and spiritual growth by providing:

- Educational support and tutoring
- Health services and nutritious lunches
- Parenting classes for mothers and fathers

All of these services and activities are informed by Christian values and principles.

For more information on sponsoring a Potter's House child, visit pottershouse.org.gt/sponsorship or email sponsorship@ pottershouse.org.gt.

Appendix C

2020 – 2025 Strategic Plan

Potter's House
Association

Guatemala, March 2020

Introduction

We are thankful to God for the completion of our first strategic plan in 2019, which was yet another milestone in the ministry. We are witnesses of God's faithfulness and presence in the expansion process of the ministry to other regions in the country and through innovative strategies to combat poverty. He enabled us to systematize the experience and our model as a Christ-centered model while we implemented the plans.

The implementing team is thankful to God for the transformation process experienced. We are very appreciative of having been invited to be a part of the expansion of His Kingdom in Guatemala.

This next stage, now that the ministry has presence in three regions in the country, has its new strategic plan. We are expectant! Once again, this has been a team effort; we have dedicated time to prayer, reflection, research and planning. This second plan seeks to continue honoring God by proclaiming the good news to the needy as its main pillar for the transformation and consolidation of the ministry in the three regions.

We have placed in God's hands the information contained in this document. We pray for His guidance and presence.

As you read this document, we invite you to ask God where and how to join in the work of God for these Treasures in our beloved Guatemala.

From all of us in the Potter's House team,

Héctor Rivas

Executive Director

Mission

Potter's House is a Christ-centered organization that fights poverty in Guatemala by promoting a personal relationship with God through Jesus Christ while deploying holistic development programs that focus on at-risk children and youth.

Vision

That every beneficiary child and youth, through their personal relationship with God, will reach the maturity they need to pursue their own holistic development and will contribute in the fight against poverty by influencing their family, community and nation.

Organizational Principles

Bible principles govern the Kingdom of God. In all these years of service, Potter's House has learned there are five principles that govern our values, our service perspective and our actions. They are the following:

Love

Patience

Faith and Hope

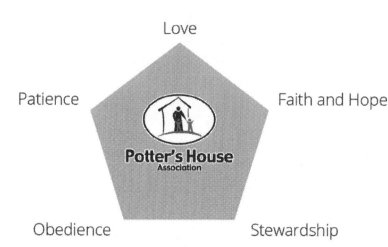

Obedience

Stewardship

1. LOVE: It is the firm belief in the love of God and for our neighbor. It is the correct motivation to love and serve our neighbor. It is the acceptance that each of us has received different talents and roles from God and is loved by Him.

Biblical foundation:
Matthew 22:37-40, 1 John 4:7-21
Exodus 20:1-17, Colossians 3:14
1 Corinthians 13:1-7, Matthew 7:21-23, Romans 13:10

2. FAITH AND HOPE: Our hope is in God at all times—good or bad. Faith is the assuredness that comes from knowing God intimately and experiencing Him as Sovereign, a strong and righteous God, great in love and mercies; He has plans for good, to give us a future and a hope.

Biblical foundation:
1 Corinthians 13:13
Jeremiah 29:11
John 10:10

3. STEWARDSHIP: Everything belongs to God and He gives to each according to their abilities. We know and live by this belief: we are God's stewards and we are accountable to Him for what He has entrusted in our care.

Biblical foundation:
Matthew 25: 14-30
1 Peter 4:10
1 Corinthians 4:1,2

4. OBEDIENCE: It is doing the will of God. Living out this principle enables us to act in obedience to God's call for us.

When we obey His instructions, we focus on the right priorities. These actions produce joy and deliver us from jealousy and pointless comparison. We accomplish what God has required us to do.

We live for God—He is the audience we are interested in pleasing. This certainty gives us courage and the certainty that the work will come to pass by His hand.

When we live in His might we honor Him with what we do and what He does through us.

Living this way—as with the vine and the branches—honors God through the results of the ministry, as they attest to His presence and might.

Biblical foundation:
Psalms 139:16
Joshua 1:7-9
Jeremiah 1:4-5
Matthew 28:19-20
2 Corinthians 9:13

5. PATIENCE: It is our strength in adversity and in difficult cases. It is the ability to wait and remain faithful to the call that comes from believing in the promises of God, in the assurance of Who He is, and in His transforming work in our life.

Biblical foundation:
Galatians 6:9, Habakkuk 3:17-19
Colossians 3:12-13, Ephesians 4:2

Values

Service to the Poor

Community & Nation

Leadership

Transformation

Reliability

Potter's House
Association

Feasibility

Long-term relationships

Adaptabiility   Stewardship

STRATEGIC FACTORS

1. IMPACT: Impact is the Christ-centered change driven by PHA in the target group. It is intentional, effective, measurable and efficient. Its purpose is to enable the person to progressively mature in his/her comprehensive development. Through a SWOT and organizational analysis, we identified the two strategic areas that are foundational to PHA's impact:

A. EIGHT TYPES OF POVERTY: The theory of Eight Forms of Poverty created by PHA in 1995 is still valid. Compared to other perspectives, this is an accurate theory useful in understanding the problem of poverty and in planning effective strategies in its combat. The Eight Forms of Poverty are:

B. ASSISTENTIALISM AND RELIGIOSITY: Our work experience and case studies show that assistentialism (poverty of the will) and religiosity (spiritual poverty) are factors that affect a person's transformation process. PHA defines both concepts as follows:

Religiosity: "It is the action of keeping and observing the external, traditional, liturgical or legal aspects of a religion as the only thing needed and indispensable to please God."

Assistentialism: "An aid mechanism that disregards the causes that lead a person to poverty; it does not consider the person's individual attributes or learning ability to permanently step out of that condition."

2. SUSTAINABILITY: It is the optimal balance of strategic, organizational and financial factors that allow PHA's impact initiatives to last in time. It includes two strategic areas:

A. REVENUES THROUGH DONATIONS: A country approach was used to determine that revenues and donor-based revenues need to increase while reducing the distance between PHA-Partner and through keeping relevant, constant and consistent communication.

B. ALTERNATIVE REVENUE SOURCES: We see an opportunity to generate revenue through strategic businesses in the face of the constant emergence of organizations in the non-profit sector and current global trends.

3. GROWTH: The increase in PHA's organizational capabilities to produce the longest lasting impact possible in the target group with the resources available.

A. COUNTRY PLATFORM: For 25 years PHA's work focused mainly on the families living in the areas around the garbage dump in Guatemala City. In the last seven years, PHA has consistently and conservatively become an organization with a country platform. Consequently, PHA now has presence in communities in five departments and the capability to expand in the future.

B. EXPANSION: Growth to communities in the vicinity of regional offices and community centers is feasible with a country platform.

ORGANIZATIONAL STRATEGIES

1. WORK MODEL (3-1-3 STRATEGY)

The model consists of:

3-1-3
STRATEGY

Potter's House
Association

Three Transformation Stages
Develop, Empower and Multiply

Community Center: Physical places strategically located in Guatemala that are equipped to enable the DEM (Develop-Empower-Multiply) transformation process, with special emphasis on children and youth in poverty.

Three areas of impact: Family, community, nation

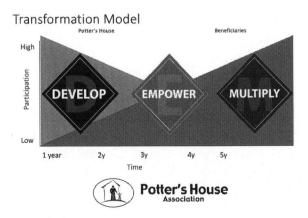

C. EXPANSION PROCESS: The process that enables us to replicate PHA's work model customized to other communities in the country in order to combat poverty. It is implemented in four stages:

1. Scouting and research
2. Verification and reconnaissance
3. Pilot projects
4. Community center establishment creation

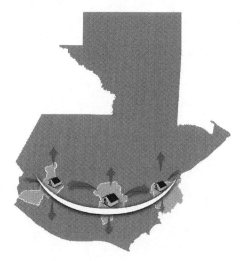

"I am the vine; you are the branches. If you remain in me and I in you, you will bear much fruit; apart from me you can do nothing."—John 15:5

B. NETWORKING AND PARTNERSHIPS: Potter's House understands that in order to experience the expansion of the Kingdom of God in our beloved Guatemala, the support of others is needed. These individuals and institutions need to be willing to be part of the transformation and development of the children and youth we serve. We are aware that we do ministry along with those who participate with us.

STRATEGIC OBJECTIVES

The following objectives are needed to implement the 2020-2025 strategic plan:

IMPACT

1. **Foster** actions that encourage the participation and decisions of the beneficiary as the protagonist of his/her own comprehensive development. (TO COMBAT ASSISTENTIALISM)

2. **Encourage** the beginning of a personal relationship with God and the practice of Bible principles and values to evidence permanent changes in the relationship with his/her family, community and nation. (TO COMBAT RELIGIOSITY)

SUSTAINABILITY

3. **Procure** the required resources for the organization by cultivating relationships that are long-term, participatory, transformational and Christ-centered with all our national and international contacts. (TO BUILD RELATIONS)

4. **Contribute** to the financial sustainability of the organization through alternative revenue sources.

GROWTH

5. **Strengthen** the existing country platform, mainly in the Central, East and West regions. This will be evidenced in the population served, the work model and the organizational systems and structure

SPECIFIC OBJECTIVES

REGIONS

1. **Establish** the West Regional Office to focus our work model in the departments of San Marcos, Totonicapán and Quetzaltenango. (West)

2. **Encourage** the well-being of Treasures, families and communities in the Chiquimula Department by reducing food insecurity and by developing their abilities. (East)

3. **Guide** the Treasures in the process of becoming independent in academic, nutritional, work-related and economic aspects.

COUNTRY PLATFORM

4. **Expand** the organization's contacts network locally and internationally. (PARTNERSHIP DEVELOPMENT)

5. **Contribute** to the financial sustainability of the organization through fundraising and business actions. (INNOVATION)

6. **Empower** participants to actively monitor best practices on security. (OPERATIONS)

7. **Prepare** a high-performance team of collaborators to honor God in the way they live and serve. (STAFF DEVELOPMENT)

8. **Automate** the administrative, financial and accounting systems in order to have transparent, reliable, timely, secure and useable information. (FINANCIAL MANAGEMENT)

About the Author

Gladys Acuña Güitz, a native of Guatemala City, has spent more than 34 years serving the Lord through *Asociación Casa del Alfarero* (Potter's House Association) in Guatemala.

When she did a favor for some friends on Christmas Eve in 1986 by grudgingly delivering blankets to people who lived in and around a huge garbage dump, she had no idea that this pocket of extreme poverty even existed in her city. She was reluctant to go there, and she swore to herself that she would never return. But God called her to return, and she soon began to love the poor and ultimately committed her life to serving what she came to believe were God's "Treasures" in the dump community.

Her passion is to share what she has learned about constructive ways to serve the poor and encourage others to love them because God has a special heart for them.

Hidden Treasure, written with Betsy Ahl, is her first book. In it she describes how the Lord called her to serve the scavengers of the Guatemala City garbage dump community and led her to co-found Potter's House Association in 1986. She shares how it felt to find her calling in a garbage dump among the Treasures she would come to love as she opens her heart to share struggles and misconceptions, as well as a deeper understanding of God, herself, and others.

Potter's House, a Christ-centered organization that fights poverty in Guatemala by promoting a personal relationship with God through Jesus Christ while deploying holistic development programs that focus on at-risk children and youth, has been a force for good in Guatemala since 1986. The ministry now seeks to replicate its successful model in other parts of the country, equipping local leaders to fight poverty and live out the Gospel.

Her website is **GladysGuitz.com.**

Made in the USA
Middletown, DE
21 May 2021